P9-DVQ-492

NorthStar 3

LISTENING AND SPEAKING

THIRD EDITION

AUTHORS
Helen S. Solórzano
Jennifer P. L. Schmidt

SERIES EDITORS
Frances Boyd
Carol Numrich

PEARSON
Longman

NorthStar: Listening and Speaking Level 3, Third Edition

Copyright © 2009, 2004, 1998 by Pearson Education, Inc.
All rights reserved.

No part of this publication may be reproduced, stored in a retrieval system, or transmitted in any form, or by any means, electronic, mechanical, photocopying, recording, or otherwise, without the prior permission of the publisher.

Pearson Education, 10 Bank Street, White Plains, NY 10606

Contributor credit: Linda Lane, American Language Program at Columbia University, authored and edited PRONUNCIATION material for *NorthStar: Listening and Speaking Levels 1–5, Third Edition.*

Staff credits: The people who made up the **NorthStar: Listening and Speaking Level 3, Third Edition** team, representing editorial, production, design, and manufacturing, are Aerin Csigay, Dave Dickey, Ann France, Shelley Gazes, Gosia Jaros-White, Dana Klinek, Melissa Leyva, Sherry Preiss, Robert Ruvo, Debbie Sistino, and Paula Van Ells.

Cover art: Silvia Rojas/Getty Images
Text composition: ElectraGraphics, Inc.
Text font: 11.5/13 Minion
Credits: See page 214.

Library of Congress Cataloging-in-Publication Data

Northstar. Listening and speaking. — 3rd ed.
    4 v. ; cm.
  Rev. ed. of: Northstar / Robin Mills and Helen Solórzano, 2nd. ed. 2004.
  The third edition of the Northstar series has been expanded to 4 separate volumes. Each level is in a separate volume with different contributing authors.
    Includes bibliographical references.
    Contents: Level 2: Basic Low Intermediate /Laurie Frazier, Robin Mills — Level 3: Intermediate / Helen Solórzano, Jennifer P.L. Schmidt — Level 4: High Intermediate / Tess Ferree, Kim Sanabria — Level 5: Advanced / Sherry Preiss.
    ISBN-13: 978-0-13-240988-9 (pbk. : student text bk. level 2 : alk. paper)
    ISBN-10: 0-13-240988-7 (pbk. : student text bk. level 2 : alk. paper)
    ISBN-13: 978-0-13-613313-1 (pbk. : student text bk. level 3 : alk. paper)
    ISBN-10: 0-13-613313-4 (pbk. : student text bk. level 3 : alk. paper)
    [etc.]
  1. English language—Textbooks for foreign speakers. 2. English language—Spoken English—Problems, exercises, etc. 3. Listening—Problems, exercises, etc. I. Mills, Robin, 1964– Northstar. II. Title: Listening and speaking.
  PE1128.N674 2008
  428.2'4—dc22

            2008024491

ISBN-10: 0-13-613313-4
ISBN-13: 978-0-13-613313-1

Printed in the United States of America
8 9 10—V011—13 12 11

CONTENTS

WELCOME TO NORTHSTAR

THIRD EDITION

NorthStar, now in its third edition, motivates students to succeed in their **academic** as well as **personal** language goals.

For each of the five levels, the two strands—*Reading and Writing* and *Listening and Speaking*—provide a fully integrated approach for students and teachers.

WHAT IS SPECIAL ABOUT THE THIRD EDITION?

NEW THEMES

New themes and **updated content**—presented in a **variety of genres**, including literature and lectures, and in **authentic reading and listening selections**—challenge students intellectually.

ACADEMIC SKILLS

More purposeful **integration of critical thinking** and an enhanced focus on **academic skills** such as inferencing, synthesizing, note taking, and test taking help students develop strategies for **success** in the **classroom** and on **standardized tests**. A **culminating productive task** galvanizes content, language, and **critical thinking skills**.

➤ In the *Listening and Speaking* strand, a **structured approach** gives students opportunities for **more extended and creative oral practice**, for example, presentations, simulations, debates, case studies, and public service announcements.

➤ In the *Reading and Writing* strand, a new, **fully integrated writing section** leads students through the **writing process** with engaging writing assignments focusing on various rhetorical modes.

NEW DESIGN

Full **color pages** with more **photos, illustrations, and graphic organizers** foster student engagement and make the content and activities come alive.

MyNorthStarLab

MyNorthStarLab, an easy-to-use **online learning and assessment program**, offers:

➤ Unlimited access to reading and listening selections and DVD segments.

➤ Focused test preparation to help students succeed on international exams such as TOEFL® and IELTS®. Pre- and post-unit assessments improve results by providing individualized instruction, instant feedback, and personalized study plans.

➤ Original activities that support and extend the *NorthStar* program. These include pronunciation practice using voice recording tools, and activities to build note taking skills and academic vocabulary.

➤ Tools that save time. These include a flexible gradebook and authoring features that give teachers control of content and help them track student progress.

THE NORTHSTAR APPROACH

The *NorthStar* series is based on **current research in language acquisition** and on the **experiences of teachers and curriculum designers**. Five principles guide the *NorthStar* approach.

PRINCIPLES

1 The more profoundly students are stimulated intellectually and emotionally, the more language they will use and retain.

The thematic organization of *NorthStar* promotes intellectual and emotional stimulation. The 50 sophisticated themes in *NorthStar* present intriguing topics such as recycled fashion, restorative justice, personal carbon footprints, and microfinance. The authentic content engages students, links them to language use outside of the classroom, and encourages personal expression and critical thinking.

2 Students can learn both the form and content of the language.

Grammar, vocabulary, and culture are inextricably woven into the units, providing students with systematic and multiple exposures to language forms in a variety of contexts. As the theme is developed, students can express complex thoughts using a higher level of language.

3 Successful students are active learners.

Tasks are designed to be creative, active, and varied. Topics are interesting and up-to-date. Together these tasks and topics (1) allow teachers to bring the outside world into the classroom and (2) motivate students to apply their classroom learning in the outside world.

4 Students need feedback.

This feedback comes naturally when students work together practicing language and participating in open-ended opinion and inference tasks. Whole class activities invite teachers' feedback on the spot or via audio/video recordings or notes. The innovative new MyNorthStarLab gives students immediate feedback as they complete computer-graded language activities online; it also gives students the opportunity to submit writing or speaking assignments electronically to their instructor for feedback later.

5 The quality of relationships in the language classroom is important because students are asked to express themselves on issues and ideas.

The information and activities in *NorthStar* promote genuine interaction, acceptance of differences, and authentic communication. By building skills and exploring ideas, the exercises help students participate in discussions and write essays of an increasingly complex and sophisticated nature.

THE NORTHSTAR UNIT

1 FOCUS ON THE TOPIC

This section introduces students to the unifying theme
of the listening selections.

> **PREDICT** and **SHARE INFORMATION** foster interest in the unit topic and help
> students develop a personal connection to it.
>
> **BACKGROUND** AND **VOCABULARY** activities provide students with tools for
> understanding the first listening selection. Later in the unit, students review
> this vocabulary and learn related idioms, collocations, and word forms. This
> helps them explore content and expand their written and spoken language.

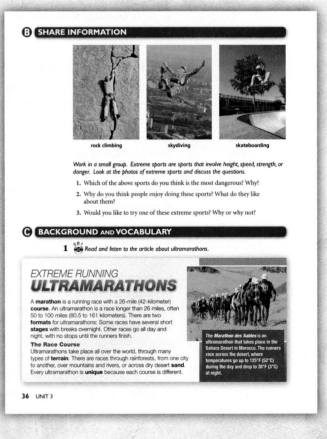

② FOCUS ON LISTENING

This section focuses on understanding two contrasting listening selections.

> **LISTENING ONE** is a radio report, interview, lecture, or other genre that addresses the unit topic. In levels 1 to 3, listenings are based on authentic materials. In levels 4 and 5, all the listenings are authentic.
>
> **LISTEN FOR MAIN IDEAS** and **LISTEN FOR DETAILS** are comprehension activities that lead students to an understanding and appreciation of the first selection.
>
> The **MAKE INFERENCES** activity prompts students to "listen between the lines," move beyond the literal meaning, exercise critical thinking skills, and understand the listening on a more academic level. Students follow up with pair or group work to discuss topics in the **EXPRESS OPINIONS** section.

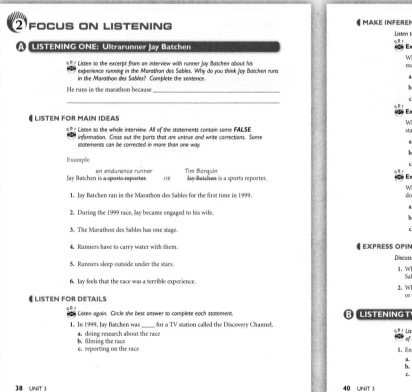

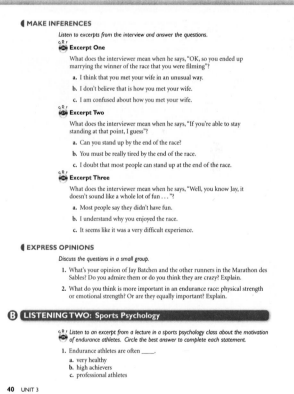

LISTENING TWO offers another perspective on the topic and is usually another genre. Again, in levels 1 to 3, the listenings are based on authentic materials and in levels 4 and 5, they are authentic. This second listening is followed by an activity that challenges students to question ideas they formed about the first listening, and to use appropriate language skills to analyze and explain their ideas.

INTEGRATE LISTENINGS ONE AND TWO presents culminating activities. Students are challenged to take what they have learned, organize the information, and synthesize it in a meaningful way. Students practice skills that are essential for success in authentic academic settings and on standardized tests.

B **LISTENING TWO: Simple Gifts**

1 *Read the information about the Shakers, an eighteenth-century religious group who chose to live simply.*

The Shakers were a religious group that formed in Britain in the 1700s. They came to the United States so they could be free to practice their religion.

The Shakers believed that simple living would make them happy and would bring them closer to God. They wore plain clothing and shared everything. They never married or had children. Men and women lived in separate houses.

The name "Shakers" came from the group's style of dancing. Dancing was an important part of Shaker religion. However, other people thought the Shaker dances were very strange.

"Simple Gifts" is a Shaker dance song written in 1848 that is still a popular folk song today.

2 🎵 *Listen to the song. Complete the song lyrics with the missing words from the box. Some words are used twice. Listen again if you need to.*

ashamed	delight	gained	~~simple~~
be	free	right	

Simple Gifts

Written by Joseph Brackett.
Performed by Kathryn Robbins.

Line

1 'Tis[1] the gift to be _____simple_____, 'tis the gift to be _____,

2 'Tis the gift to come down[2] where we ought to _____,

3 And when we find ourselves in the place just _____,

4 'Twill[3] be in the valley[4] of love and _____.

---
[1]**'tis:** it is
[2]**come down:** stop at
[3]**'twill:** it will
[4]**valley:** a low area of land between two mountains

C **INTEGRATE LISTENINGS ONE AND TWO**

◀ **STEP 1: Organize**

There are connections between the ideas in the Shaker song "Simple Gifts" and the lifestyle of the urban homesteaders. Work with a partner. Read the lines from the song. Then answer the questions.

LINES FROM "SIMPLE GIFTS"	QUESTIONS	ANSWERS FOR URBAN HOMESTEADERS
'Tis the gift to be simple.	1. What do the urban homesteaders do to lead a simple life?	they grow their own vegetables
'Tis the gift to be free.	2. In what ways are the urban homesteaders free? (What things are they free from?)	
'Tis the gift to come down where we ought to be.	3. Why is the inner city the place where the urban homesteaders want to be?	
'Twill be in the valley of love and delight.	4. What makes the urban homesteaders delighted (happy)?	

◀ **STEP 2: Synthesize**

Work with a new partner and compare your answers to the questions. Take turns reading the questions and responding by agreeing, disagreeing, or adding more information. Use the information from Step 1 and the useful language on the next page.

Example

STUDENT A: OK. Question 1 says, "What do the urban homesteaders do to lead a simple life?" Well . . . to lead a simple life the urban homesteaders grow their own vegetables.
STUDENT B: Right. They also don't use electricity.

---

③ FOCUS ON SPEAKING

This section emphasizes development of productive skills for speaking. It includes sections on vocabulary, grammar, pronunciation, functional language, and an extended speaking task.

The **VOCABULARY** section leads students from reviewing the unit vocabulary, to practicing and expanding their use of it, and then working with it—using it creatively in both this section and in the final speaking task.

Students learn useful structures for speaking in the **GRAMMAR** section, which offers a concise presentation and targeted practice. Vocabulary items are recycled here, providing multiple exposures leading to mastery. For additional practice with the grammar presented, students and teachers can consult the GRAMMAR BOOK REFERENCES at the end of the book for corresponding material in the *Focus on Grammar* and Azar series.

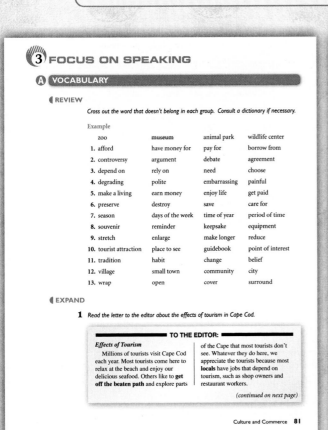

The **PRONUNCIATION** section presents both controlled and freer, communicative practice of the sounds and patterns of English. Models from the listening selections reinforce content and vocabulary. This is followed by the **FUNCTION** section where students are exposed to functional language that prepares them to express ideas on a higher level. Examples have been chosen based on frequency, variety, and usefulness for the final speaking task.

The **PRODUCTION** section gives students an opportunity to integrate the ideas, vocabulary, grammar, pronunciation, and function presented in the unit. This final speaking task is the culminating activity of the unit and gets students to exchange ideas and express opinions in sustained speaking contexts. Activities are presented in a sequence that builds confidence and fluency, and allows for more than one "try" at expression. When appropriate, students practice some presentation skills: audience analysis, organization, eye contact, or use of visuals.

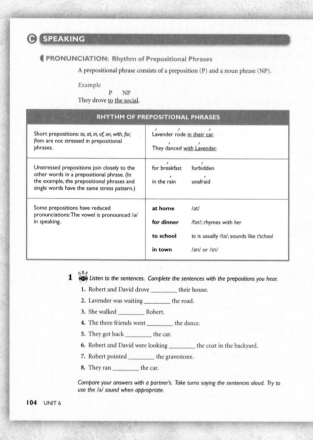

C SPEAKING

◀ PRONUNCIATION: Rhythm of Prepositional Phrases

A prepositional phrase consists of a preposition (P) and a noun phrase (NP).

Example

P   NP
They drove to the social.

RHYTHM OF PREPOSITIONAL PHRASES		
Short prepositions: *to, at, in, of, on, with, for, from* are not stressed in prepositional phrases.	Lavender rode in their car.	
	They danced with Lavender.	
Unstressed prepositions join closely to the other words in a prepositional phrase. (In the example, the prepositional phrases and single words have the same stress pattern.)	for breakfast	forbidden
	in the rain	unafraid
Some prepositions have reduced pronunciations. The vowel is pronounced /ə/ in speaking.	**at home**	/ət/
	for dinner	/fər/; rhymes with *her*
	to school	*to* is usually /tə/; sounds like *t'school*
	in town	/ən/ or /ɪn/

1 🎧 *Listen to the sentences. Complete the sentences with the prepositions you hear.*

1. Robert and David drove _____ their house.
2. Lavender was waiting _____ the road.
3. She walked _____ Robert.
4. The three friends went _____ the dance.
5. They got back _____ the car.
6. Robert and David were looking _____ the coat in the backyard.
7. Robert pointed _____ the gravestone.
8. They ran _____ the car.

Compare your answers with a partner's. Take turns saying the sentences aloud. Try to use the /ə/ sound when appropriate.

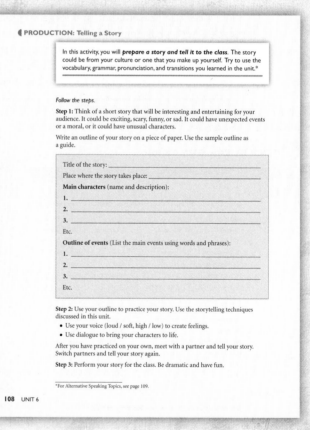

◀ PRODUCTION: Telling a Story

In this activity, you will *prepare a story and tell it to the class*. The story could be from your culture or one that you make up yourself. Try to use the vocabulary, grammar, pronunciation, and transitions you learned in the unit.*

Follow the steps.

Step 1: Think of a short story that will be interesting and entertaining for your audience. It could be exciting, scary, funny, or sad. It could have unexpected events or a moral, or it could have unusual characters.

Write an outline of your story on a piece of paper. Use the sample outline as a guide.

Title of the story: _____

Place where the story takes place: _____

Main characters (name and description):

1. _____
2. _____
3. _____

Etc.

Outline of events (List the main events using words and phrases):

1. _____
2. _____
3. _____

Etc.

Step 2: Use your outline to practice your story. Use the storytelling techniques discussed in this unit.

- Use your voice (loud / soft, high / low) to create feelings.
- Use dialogue to bring your characters to life.

After you have practiced on your own, meet with a partner and tell your story. Switch partners and tell your story again.

Step 3: Perform your story for the class. Be dramatic and have fun.

*For Alternative Speaking Topics, see page 109.

ALTERNATIVE SPEAKING TOPICS are provided at the end of the unit. They can be used as *alternatives* to the final speaking task, or as *additional* assignments. RESEARCH TOPICS tied to the theme of the unit are organized in a special section at the back of the book.

COMPONENTS

TEACHER'S MANUAL WITH ACHIEVEMENT TESTS

Each level and strand of *NorthStar* has an accompanying Teacher's Manual with step-by-step **teaching suggestions**, including unique guidance for using *NorthStar* in secondary classes. The manuals include time guidelines, expansion activities, and techniques and instructions for using MyNorthStarLab. Also included are reproducible unit-by-unit achievement **tests** of **receptive** and **productive** skills, **answer keys** to both the student book and tests, and a unit-by-unit **vocabulary** list.

EXAMVIEW

NorthStar ExamView is a stand-alone CD-ROM that allows teachers to **create and customize** their own *NorthStar* tests.

DVD

The *NorthStar* DVD has **engaging, authentic video clips**, including animation, documentaries, interviews, and biographies, that correspond to the themes in *NorthStar*. Each theme contains a three- to five-minute segment that can be used with either the *Reading and Writing* strand or the *Listening and Speaking* strand. The video clips can also be viewed in MyNorthStarLab.

COMPANION WEBSITE

The companion website, www.longman.com/northstar, includes resources for teachers, such as the **scope and sequence, correlations** to other Longman products and to state standards, and **podcasts** from the *NorthStar* authors and series editors.

MyNorthStarLab

PEARSON LONGMAN **mynorthstarlab** AVAILABLE WITH the new edition of ***NORTHSTAR***

NorthStar is now available with **MyNorthStarLab**—an easy-to-use **online** program **for students and teachers** that saves time and improves results.

➤ **STUDENTS** receive **personalized instruction** and **practice** in all four skills. Audio, video, and test preparation are all in **one** place—available **anywhere, anytime**.

➤ **TEACHERS** can take advantage of many resources including online **assessments**, a flexible **gradebook**, and **tools for monitoring student progress**.

CHECK IT OUT! GO TO www.mynorthstarlab.com FOR A PREVIEW!

TURN THE PAGE TO SEE KEY FEATURES OF **MyNorthStarLab**.

MyNorthStarLab

MyNorthStarLab supports students with **individualized instruction, feedback,** and **extra help.** A wide array of resources, including a flexible **gradebook,** helps teachers manage student progress.

The MyNorthStarLab **WELCOME** page **organizes assignments and grades,** and **facilitates communication** between students and teachers.

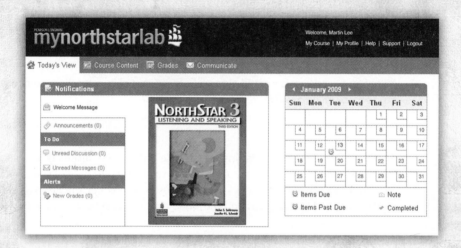

For each unit, MyNorthStarLab provides a **READINESS CHECK.**

➤ Activities **assess** student knowledge **before** beginning the unit and **follow up** with individualized instruction.

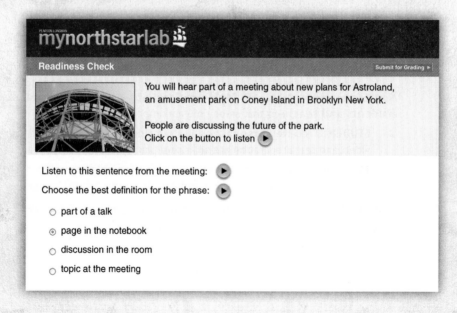

Student book material and **new** practice activities are available to students online.

➤ Students benefit from virtually unlimited **practice anywhere, anytime**.

Interaction with **Internet** and **video** materials will:

➤ Expand students' knowledge of the topic.

➤ Help students practice new vocabulary and grammar.

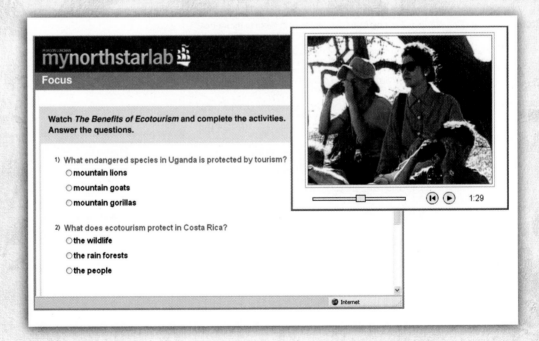

INTEGRATED SKILL ACTIVITIES in MyNorthStarLab challenge students to bring together the **language skills** and **critical thinking skills** that they have practiced throughout the unit.

Integrated Task - Read, Listen, Write   Submit for Grading ▶

THE ADVENTURE OF A LIFETIME

We at the Antarctic Travel Society <u>encourage</u> you to consider an excited guided tour of Antarctica for your next vacation.

The Antarctic Travel society carefully plans and operates tours of the Antarctic by ship. There are three trips per day leaving from <u>ports</u> in South America and Australia. Each ship carries only about 100 passengers at a time. Tours run from November through March to the ice-free areas along the coast of Antarctica.

In addition to touring the coast, our ships stop for on-land visits, which generally last for about three hours. Activities include guided sightseeing, mountain climbing, camping, <u>kayaking</u>, and <u>scuba diving</u>. For a longer stay, camping trips can also be arranged.

Our tours will give you an opportunity to experience the richness of Antarctica, including its wildlife, history, active research stations, and, most of all, its natural beauty.

Tours are <u>supervised</u> by the ship's staff. The staff generally includes <u>experts</u> in animal and sea life and other Antarctica specialists. There is generally one staff member for every 10 to 20 passengers. Theses trained and responsible individuals will help to make your visit to Antarctica safe, educational, and <u>unforgettable</u>.

READ, LISTEN AND WRITE ABOUT TOURISM IN ANTARCTICA
Read.
Read the text. Then answer the question.

According to the text, how can tourism benefit the Antarctic?

▶ **Listen.**
Click on the Play button and listen to the passage.
Use the outline to take notes as you listen.

Main idea:

Seven things that scientists study:

The effects of tourism:

Write.
Write about the potential and risks in Antarctica.
Follow the steps to prepare.

Step 1
- Review the text and your outline from the listening task.
- Write notes about the benefits and risks of tourism.

Step 2
Write for 20 minutes. Leave 5 minutes to edit your work.

The MyNorthStarLab **ASSESSMENT** tools allow instructors to customize and deliver achievement tests online.

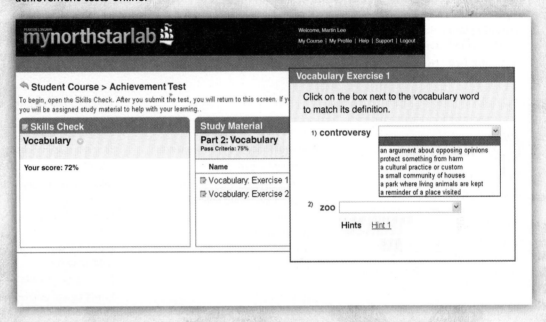

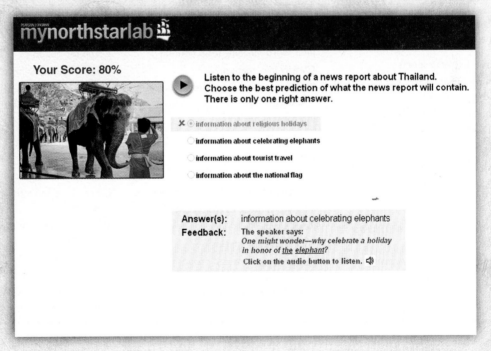

SCOPE AND SEQUENCE

UNIT	CRITICAL THINKING	LISTENING

1 **Advertising on the Air**
 	
Theme: Advertising
Listening One: *Advertising on the Air*
  A classroom lecture
Listening Two: *Negative Appeals*
  Radio ads
	Interpret and critique ads
	Infer word meaning from context
	Classify information
	Identify salient features of an ad
	Support answers with details from the listenings
	Identify intended market of ads
		Predict content
		Listen for main ideas
		Identify details
		Infer underlying messages in ads
		Organize and synthesize information from the listenings
		Identify emphasis in speech
		Evaluate effectiveness of ads
		Listen to and evaluate student ads

2 **Identity Theft**
 	
Theme: Fraud
Listening One: *Lily's Story*
  A story about personal experience with fraud
Listening Two: *Public Service Announcements*
  PSAs on identity theft prevention
	Interpret a photograph
	Infer word meaning from context
	Classify information
	Support opinions with reasons
	Choose appropriate punishments for criminal acts
	Hypothesize outcomes
		Predict content
		Listen for main ideas
		Identify details
		Infer implied meaning through intonation
		Organize and synthesize information from the listenings
		Listen for suggestions to prevent identity theft
		Listen for rhythm in speech
		Listen to and evaluate student role plays

3 **Endurance Test**
 	
Theme: Extreme sports
Listening One: *Ultrarunner Jay Batchen*
  A radio interview
Listening Two: *Sports Psychology*
  A university lecture
	Interpret photographs
	Rank extreme sports
	Infer word meaning from context
	Classify information
	Support answers with information from the listenings
	Interpret aphorisms
		Predict content
		Identify main ideas
		Listen for details
		Infer speakers' points of view
		Organize and synthesize information from the listenings
		Classify sounds

4 **Separated by the Same Language**
 	
Theme: Language
Listening One: *Accent and Identity*
  An interview
Listening Two: *Code-Switching*
  A university lecture
	Interpret a cartoon
	Identify accents
	Recognize personal bias toward accents
	Infer word meaning from context
	Read a map
	Hypothesize scenarios
	Analyze problems and propose solutions
	Hypothesize another's point of view
		Predict content
		Listen for main ideas and details
		Listen closely to interpret a speaker's emotions
		Infer attitudes about accents from statements
		Take notes on a lecture
		Identify opinions about accents
		Organize and synthesize information from the listenings

SPEAKING	VOCABULARY	GRAMMAR	PRONUNCIATION
Speculate about the content of the unit Comment on ads using new vocabulary Share personal opinions about advertising Use appropriate stress and intonation Use attention-grabbing language to promote a product Create, rehearse, and perform an ad	Use context clues to find meaning Identify parts of speech Choose word definitions	Present simple and present progressive	Highlighting words
Express and defend opinions about identity theft Conduct a role play Share personal opinions about crime Agree and disagree with statements Use strategies for keeping a conversation going Offer advice for identity theft prevention Create, practice, and perform a role play	Use context clues to find meaning Determine connotations of words Use idiomatic expressions Identify synonyms	Modals of advice	Stress in compound words
Express opinions about extreme sports Share experiences Relate personal goals Conduct an interview Discuss emotions Interpret and discuss aphorisms Create an aphorism	Use context clues to find meaning Define words Complete a crossword puzzle	Reflexive and reciprocal pronouns	Expressions with *other*
Express and defend opinions about accents Conduct an interview Play a game of *Truth or Dare* Present a plan to improve English skills Lead a group discussion Discuss solutions to a problem	Use context clues to find meaning Use idiomatic expressions	Modals of ability and possibility	*Can / Can't*

SCOPE AND SEQUENCE

UNIT	CRITICAL THINKING	LISTENING

⑤ Culture and Commerce
 	
Theme: Tourism
Listening One: *Tourist Attractions or Human Zoo?*
  A radio report
Listening Two: *Town Hall Meeting in Cape Cod*
  A recording of a town hall meeting
	Interpret a photograph
	Infer word meaning from context
	Evaluate advantages and disadvantages
	Support opinions with reasons
	Classify information
	Read a map
	Hypothesize outcomes
	Collaborate to reach a compromise
		Predict content
		Listen for main ideas and details
		Infer speakers' emotions
		Identify contrasting viewpoints in the listenings
		Organize and synthesize information from the listenings
		Categorize sounds

⑥ The Art of Storytelling
 	
Theme: Storytelling
Listening One: *Lavender*
  A story
Listening Two: *How to Tell a Story*
  A recording of a storyteller sharing his craft
	Interpret a photograph
	Infer word meaning from context
	Sequence events in a story
	Analyze storytelling techniques
	Complete an outline
	Match actions to their consequences
		Make predictions about events in a story
		Identify main events in a story
		Arrange details in a story chronologically
		Relate emotions to details in a story
		Match storytelling techniques to purposes
		Organize and synthesize information from the listenings
		Identify stress patterns in speech

⑦ Voluntary Simplicity
 	
Theme: The simple life
Listening One: *Urban Homesteaders*
  A radio report
Listening Two: *Simple Gifts*
  A traditional folk song
	Interpret photographs
	Infer word meaning from context
	Evaluate information
	Classify information
	Brainstorm ideas
	Apply information to new contexts
	Complete an outline
		Predict content
		Listen for main ideas
		Identify correct details
		Infer preferences based on statements
		Link lines from a song to details from an interview
		Listen for rhythm patterns in speech

SPEAKING	VOCABULARY	GRAMMAR	PRONUNCIATION
Agree and disagree with statements Discuss the pros and cons of tourism Talk about a tourist destination Hypothesize possible outcomes Make suggestions Participate in a simulation	Use context clues to find meaning Define words Group words with similar meaning Use idiomatic expressions	Future predictions with *if*-clauses	Words spelled with *o*
Share opinions about stories Agree and disagree with statements Create role plays Practice stress patterns in speech Use transitions to give information about events in a story Create, practice, and tell a story	Use context clues to find meaning Define words Label illustrations with new vocabulary	Infinitives of purpose	Rhythm of prepositional phrases
Express opinions about alternative lifestyles Talk about voluntary simplicity Practice agreeing and disagreeing Make analogies with target vocabulary Produce correct rhythm patterns in sentences Use descriptive language to enhance statements Create an outline Give an impromptu presentation	Use context clues to find meaning Find and use synonyms Identify variations in word meaning by context Use idiomatic expressions	Nouns and quantifiers	Noticing rhythm

SCOPE AND SEQUENCE

UNIT	CRITICAL THINKING	LISTENING
8 **Before You Say "I Do"** **Theme:** Marriage **Listening One:** *A Prenuptial Agreement* A radio talk show **Listening Two:** *Reactions to the Prenuptial Agreement* Recording of people expressing their opinions	Interpret a photograph Interpret quotations about marriage Infer word meaning from context Hypothesize another's point of view Judge the value of a prenuptial agreement Categorize information Develop arguments for and against an issue Interpret a graph	Predict content Identify main ideas Listen for details Infer speakers' points of view Organize and synthesize information from the listenings Listen for contrastive stress in speech
9 **Personal Carbon Footprint** **Theme:** Climate change **Listening One:** *Personal Carbon Footprint* A radio report **Listening Two:** *A Call to Action* A speech at a rally	Interpret illustrations Complete a survey on personal carbon footprints Understand a scientific process Infer word meaning from context Classify data Categorize information Read a map Interpret a graph	Predict content Listen for main ideas Listen for details Infer speakers' opinions Label a graph Organize and synthesize information from the listenings
10 **To Spank or Not to Spank?** **Theme:** Punishment **Listening One:** *The Spanking Debate* A radio report **Listening Two:** *Parents' Rights versus Children's Rights* A university lecture	Interpret an illustration Infer word meaning from context Identify arguments for and against spanking Classify information Conduct a survey Evaluate effectiveness of arguments	Predict content Determine speakers' points of view Identify supporting ideas Infer speakers' opinions Take notes on a lecture Organize and synthesize information from the listenings Identify end sounds

SPEAKING	VOCABULARY	GRAMMAR	PRONUNCIATION
Speculate about the content of the unit Discuss quotations about marriage Express and defend opinions about marriage Agree and disagree with statements Use word stress to change meaning Use transitions Prepare and perform an oral presentation	Use context clues to find meaning Define words	Comparatives and equatives	Contrastive stress
Speculate about the content of the unit Discuss results of a survey Express and defend opinions Agree and disagree with statements Conduct a fluency line drill based on information from the listenings Interrupt politely and hold the floor Participate in a seminar about climate change	Use context clues to find meaning Define words Identify and use correct word forms	Modals of necessity	Intonation—Are you finished?
Speculate about the content of the unit Share personal experiences Express and defend opinions Agree and disagree with statements Discuss corporal punishment Use language to express confidence Participate in a debate	Use context clues to find meaning Define words Use idiomatic expressions Find and use synonyms	Present perfect tense	Final s and z

ACKNOWLEDGMENTS

It has been a pleasure to work with the many talented and dedicated people who supported the creation of this book. A special thank you goes to Frances Boyd and Carol Numrich, whose evolving vision for *NorthStar* continues to keep the series fresh and exciting, and to our editorial team, including Sherry Preiss, Debbie Sistino, Gosia Jaros-White, and Dana Klinek, for their support and thoughtful feedback during the writing process.

Many thanks also to producers Tim Borquin, Karen Brown, Eric Molinsky, Kurt Nickish, and Kathryn Robbins for their creative and thought-provoking audio pieces, and to Jay Batchen, "Lily," and the late Jackie Torrence for sharing their stories with us.

And finally, we thank our husbands, Roy Solórzano and David Schmidt, and our children, Alonzo, Lucia, Christina, and Andrew for their patience and support throughout the writing process.

Helen S. Solórzano
Jennifer P.L. Schmidt

Reviewers

For the comments and insights they graciously offered to help shape the direction of the Third Edition of *NorthStar*, the publisher would like to thank the following reviewers and institutions.

Gail August, Hostos Community College; **Anne Bachmann**, Clackamas Community College; **Aegina Barnes**, York College, CUNY; **Dr. Sabri Bebawi**, San Jose Community College; **Kristina Beckman**, John Jay College; **Jeff Bellucci**, Kaplan Boston; **Nathan Blesse**, Human International Academy; **Alan Brandman**, Queens College; **Laila Cadavona-Dellapasqua**, Kaplan; **Amy Cain**, Kaplan; **Nigel Caplan**, Michigan State University; **Alzira Carvalho**, Human International Academy, San Diego; **Chao-Hsun (Richard) Cheng**, Wenzao Ursuline College of Languages; **Mu-hua (Yolanda) Chi**, Wenzao Ursuline College of Languages; **Liane Cismowski**, Olympic High School; **Shauna Croft**, MESLS; **Misty Crooks**, Kaplan; **Amanda De Loera**, Kaplan English Programs; **Jennifer Dobbins**, New England School of English; **Luis Dominguez**, Angloamericano; **Luydmila Drgaushanskaya**, ASA College; **Dilip Dutt**, Roxbury Community College; **Christie Evenson**, Chung Dahm Institute; **Patricia Frenz-Belkin**, Hostos Community College, CUNY; **Christiane Galvani**, Texas Southern University; **Joanna Ghosh**, University of Pennsylvania; **Cristina Gomes**, Kaplan Test Prep; **Kristen Grinager**, Lincoln High School; **Janet Harclerode**, Santa Monica College; **Carrell Harden**, HCCS, Gulfton Campus; **Connie Harney**, Antelope Valley College; **Ann Hilborn**, ESL Consultant in Houston; **Barbara Hockman**, City College of San Francisco; **Margaret Hodgson**, NorQuest College; **Paul Hong**, Chung Dahm Institute; **Wonki Hong**, Chung Dahm Institute; **John House**, Iowa State University; **Polly Howlett**, Saint Michael's College; **Arthur Hui**, Fullerton College; **Nina Ito**, CSU, Long Beach; **Scott Jenison**, Antelope Valley College; **Hyunsook Jeong**, Keimyung University; **Mandy Kama**, Georgetown University; **Dale Kim**, Chung Dahm Institute; **Taeyoung Kim**, Keimyung University; **Woo-hyung Kim**, Keimyung University; **Young Kim**, Chung Dahm Institute; **Yu-kyung Kim**, Sunchon National University; **John Kostovich**, Miami Dade College; **Albert Kowun**, Fairfax, VA; **David Krise**, Michigan State University; **Cheri (Young Hee) Lee**, ReadingTownUSA English Language Institute; **Eun-Kyung Lee**, Chung Dahm Institute; **Sang Hyock Lee**, Keimyung University; **Debra Levitt**, SMC; **Karen Lewis**, Somerville, MA; **Chia-Hui Liu**, Wenzao Ursuline College of Languages; **Gennell Lockwood**, Seattle, WA; **Javier Lopez Anguiano**, Colegio Anglo Mexicano de Coyoacan; **Mary March**, Shoreline Community College; **Susan Matson**, ELS Language Centers; **Ralph McClain**, Embassy CES Boston; **Veronica McCormack**, Roxbury Community College; **Jennifer McCoy**, Kaplan; **Joseph McHugh**, Kaplan; **Cynthia McKeag Tsukamoto**, Oakton Community College; **Paola Medina**, Texas Southern University; **Christine Kyung-ah Moon**, Seoul, Korea; **Margaret Moore**, North Seattle Community College; **Michelle Moore**, Madison English as a Second Language School; **David Motta**, Miami University; **Suzanne Munro**, Clackamas Community College; **Elena Nehrbecki**, Hudson County CC; **Kim Newcomer**, University of Washington; **Melody Nightingale**, Santa Monica College; **Patrick Northover**, Kaplan Test and Prep; **Sarah Oettle**, Kaplan, Sacramento; **Shirley Ono**, Oakton Community College; **Maria Estela Ortiz Torres**, C. Anglo Mexicano de Coyoac'an; **Suzanne Overstreet**, West Valley College; **Linda Ozarow**, West Orange High School; **Ileana Porges-West**, Miami Dade College, Hialeah Campus; **Megan Power**, ILCSA; **Alison Robertson**, Cypress College; **Ma. Del Carmen Romero**, Universidad del Valle de Mexico; **Nina Rosen**, Santa Rosa Junior College; **Daniellah Salario**, Kaplan; **Joel Samuels**, Kaplan New York City; **Babi Sarapata**, Columbia University ALP; **Donna Schaeffer**, University of Washington; **Lynn Schneider**, City College of San Francisco; **Errol Selkirk**, New School University; **Amity Shook**, Chung Dahm Institute; **Lynn Stafford-Yilmaz**, Bellevue Community College; **Lynne Ruelaine Stokes**, Michigan State University; **Henna Suh**, Chung Dahm Institute; **Sheri Summers**, Kaplan Test Prep; **Martha Sutter**, Kent State University; **Becky Tarver Chase**, MESLS; **Lisa Waite-Trago**, Michigan State University; **Carol Troy**, Da-Yeh University; **Luci Tyrell**, Embassy CES Fort Lauderdale; **Yong-Hee Uhm**, Myongii University; **Debra Un**, New York University; **José Vazquez**, The University of Texas Pan American; **Hollyahna Vettori**, Santa Rosa Junior College; **Susan Vik**, Boston University; **Sandy Wagner**, Fort Lauderdale High School; **Joanne Wan**, ASC English; **Pat Wiggins**, Clackamas Community College; **Heather Williams**, University of Pennsylvania; **Carol Wilson-Duffy**, Michigan State University; **Kailin Yang**, Kaohsing Medical University; **Ellen Yaniv**, Boston University; **Samantha Young**, Kaplan Boston; **Yu-san Yu**, National Sun Yat-sen University; **Ann Zaaijer**, West Orange High School

UNIT 1

Advertising on the Air

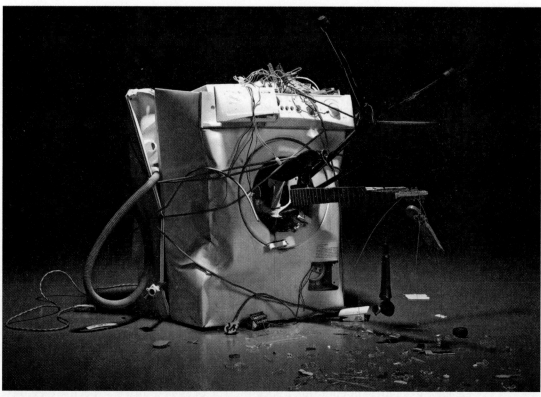

①FOCUS ON THE TOPIC

A PREDICT

Discuss the questions with the class.

1. Look at the advertisement. What product do you think this company is advertising? (After you guess, look at the answer below.)

2. Do you think this is a good ad? Would you buy the product? Why or why not?

3. Look at the title of the unit. What kind of advertising do you think this unit will be about?

Answer: a pain medication

Work in a small group. Describe an ad you have seen or heard recently. Discuss whether you liked the ad and why. Use the questions to guide your discussion.

Did the ad have ... ?
- a funny situation
- a good song
- nice-looking people
- a famous person
- information about the product
- (other)

1 ^{CD 7}❷ *Read and listen to the article about advertising from a business textbook.*

Advertising Today

Introduction to Advertising

Advertising is a way companies get **consumers** to buy their products. Advertisers often **rely on** TV commercials and magazine ads to sell their products. However, with so many ads, it's difficult for advertisers to **get our attention**. For this reason, they often look for new, more **effective** ways to sell their products. One popular **technique** is the use of **sound effects**, such as a crying baby or breaking glass, to make us listen. Another technique is "product placement." For example, an actor in a movie might drink a specific type of soda or drive a specific type of car. Advertisers hope that this will give consumers a positive feeling about the product so they will decide to buy it.

When advertisers create their ads, they also think about who will buy their product most often. They think about many **factors**, such as the ages or genders of the consumers. Then they choose different **appeals** for different groups of consumers. For example, advertisers may use a **humorous** appeal to sell a children's product. In ads for adults, advertisers may **emphasize** other things, such as price and quality.

2 *Circle the correct answer to complete each statement.*

1. A **consumer** is someone who _____.
   a. sells a product   b. buys a product

2. When an advertiser **relies on** only TV ads to sell a product, the advertiser _____.
   a. puts ads on TV, radio, and magazines   b. puts ads on TV but nowhere else

3. When an ad **gets our attention**, we _____.
   a. notice it   b. forget about it

4. An **effective** ad is an ad that _____.
   a. sells a lot of products   b. is expensive to make

5. An advertising **technique** is _____.
   a. a way to sell a product   b. a kind of advertisement

6. An example of a **sound effect** is _____.
   a. a picture of a car   b. the noise of a car

7. When buying a car, an important **factor** to think about is _____.
   a. the headlights   b. the price

8. An example of an advertising **appeal** is _____.
   a. television   b. humor

9. People often _____ when they see a **humorous** movie.
   a. laugh   b. cry

10. Many ads **emphasize** a product's low price because the cost is _____.
    a. especially important   b. less important than other things

2 FOCUS ON LISTENING

A LISTENING ONE: Advertising on the Air

CD 1 *You will hear a lecture from a business course on advertising. Listen to the*
3 beginning of the lecture. What is the professor going to discuss? Complete the
sentence.

The lecture will be about . . .

_____

CD 1
🔘 *Listen to the lecture. Circle the best answer to complete each statement.*

1. The lecture is about _____ appeals in advertising.
   a. informational
   b. emotional
   c. international

2. The professor gives examples of _____ ads.
   a. humorous
   b. musical
   c. negative

3. According to the professor, the ads are effective because they _____ about the products.
   a. include famous people's opinions
   b. give information
   c. make us feel good

4. The ads are also effective because _____.
   a. we hear them many times
   b. the products are well-known
   c. they get our attention

◖ LISTEN FOR DETAILS

CD 1
🔘 *Listen again. Fill in the missing information in the notes taken by a student in a business class.*

Intro to Advertising

Last Week: __informational__ appeals

- give consumers _____ about a product

  e.g.,[1] price, _____

This Week: emotional appeals

- feelings

- _____ (happiness, love) or negative (_____,

  embarrassment)

- common, effective _____

---

[1] e.g.: for example

- _____ often makes the sale, not _____

Most common appeal = _____

    e.g., Doggie Delight - dog _____

      - funny voice, sound effects

      - not much _____ about the product

Effective:

  1. "Feel-good" factor = gives us _____ about the
     product

  2. _____ = advertisers' #1 problem

    e.g., Neighbors' Bank

      - humor can be used with _____ products

◖ MAKE INFERENCES

Listen again to the ads. What does the advertiser assume about the consumers who will hear these ads? Circle the best answer to complete each statement.

ᶜ ᴰ ₇
6 **Ad 1: Doggie Delight**

The advertiser thinks the consumers want _____.

  a. cheap dog food
  b. a happy dog
  c. a dog who listens and obeys

ᶜ ᴰ ₇
7 **Ad 2: Neighbors' Bank**

The advertiser thinks the consumers want _____.

  a. a bank with personal service
  b. a bank with affordable service (no fees)
  c. a bank that's close to home

Discuss your answers in small groups. Explain your choices with examples from the ads.

◖ **EXPRESS OPINIONS**

Work in a small group. Complete the activities.

1 *Rate the ads from Listening One using the scale. Explain your opinion.*

Doggie Delight

Very humorous	1	2	3	4	Not humorous
Easy to remember	1	2	3	4	Hard to remember
Very effective	1	2	3	4	Not effective

Neighbors' Bank

Very humorous	1	2	3	4	Not humorous
Easy to remember	1	2	3	4	Hard to remember
Very effective	1	2	3	4	Not effective

2 *Imagine a magazine advertisement for Doggie Delight and Neighbors' Bank. How would the print ads be different from the radio ads? Could the print ads use the same emotional appeals? Why or why not?*

B **LISTENING TWO: Negative Appeals**

The ads in Listening One focused on humor, a positive emotion. In Listening Two, you will hear ads that use negative emotions.

CD 1 *Listen to the ads and complete the chart. Write down the product and choose a*
⑧ *negative emotional appeal from the box. Then write down the sound effects (sounds and voices) the advertiser uses to get our attention.*

anger	confusion	embarrassment	fear	stress

AD	PRODUCT	EMOTIONAL APPEAL	SOUND EFFECTS
1. Thief Buster	car security system		
2. Sunny Resorts			
3. White Bright			

◀ **STEP 1: Organize**

Work with a partner. Look at the list of key ideas from the lecture. Explain the meaning of each idea and write down an example ad from Listenings One and Two.

KEY IDEAS	MEANING	EXAMPLE ADS
Informational appeal	gives information to consumers about the product	Thief Buster
Emotional appeal		
Positive appeal		
Negative appeal		
Humorous appeal		
Getting a consumer's attention		
The "feel-good" factor		

◀ **STEP 2: Synthesize**

Work with a partner. Discuss the example ads you listed in the chart. Use the information from Step 1.

1. What advertising appeal is used?

2. How does it get the consumer's attention?

3. Does it use the "feel-good" factor? If so, what is it?

③ FOCUS ON SPEAKING

A VOCABULARY

◀ REVIEW

Complete the sentences with appropriate words and phrases.

1. **affordable / factors / humorous**

   _____ ads can make us laugh and remember a product.

   However, when we decide to buy something, we think about more important

   _____, such as cost: Is the product

   _____?

2. **rely on / sound effects / techniques**

   Radio uses different advertising _____ from TV.

   _____ are more important on the radio because we have to

   _____ our hearing to get information about the product.

3. **get our attention / consumers / effective**

   It is clear that advertising affects what _____ buy.

   _____ ads _____ and make us

   remember the product.

4. **emphasizes / emotional / negative**

   Advertisers know that people often make _____ decisions

   about buying a product. That's why the Thief Buster ad

   _____ the _____ things that can happen

   if you don't have the product, such as having your car stolen.

1 *Read the information from an advertising website.*

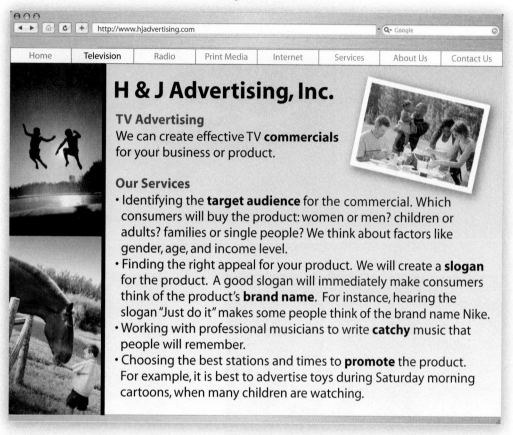

2 *Circle the correct answer to complete each statement.*

1. A **commercial** is an ad _____.
   a. in a magazine or newspaper   **b.** on radio or TV

2. A **target audience** is a group of _____ who may want a product.
   a. consumers   **b.** advertisers

3. A **slogan** is _____.
   a. a saying about a product   **b.** an opinion about a product

4. A **brand name** is the name of _____.
   a. a product   **b.** an advertising technique

5. A **catchy** ad is an ad that _____.
   a. is easy to forget   **b.** is easy to remember

6. To **promote** a product means to _____.
   a. help the product be successful   **b.** test the product

Work in a small group. Look at the ads and discuss the questions. Use the vocabulary from the box in your discussion.

Automobile

Skin care product

Laundry soap

1. Who is the target audience?

2. What is the ad saying about the product?

3. What techniques are used to get our attention? (e.g., a slogan)

4. What makes the ad effective?

brand name	emotional	negative
catchy	emphasize	positive
consumers	factor	promote
effective	humorous	rely on
	informational	

1 Look at the print ad for Sunny Resorts. Underline the simple present verbs and circle the present progressive verbs.

TYPICAL DAY

On a typical day, Martin is at work. He sits in his office all day. His phone rings constantly. He gets hundreds of e-mails. His computer usually doesn't work. His boss complains all day. He doesn't have time to take a break, so he's always tired. He hates his job.

SUNNY RESORTS DAY

Today Martin is enjoying his vacation at Sunny Resorts. He's lying on the beach and sipping a cold drink. His phone isn't ringing, and instead of checking his e-mail, he's reading a book. He remembers the office as a bad dream. He sees nothing but blue skies and sunshine. He has all the time he needs. He loves it here.

Sunny Resorts
You deserve a vacation.

SIMPLE PRESENT AND PRESENT PROGRESSIVE	
I. Use the **simple present** to state a fact or to tell about something that happens regularly.	Martin **works** in an office. Martin **sits** in his office every day.
Use the simple present with adverbs of frequency. (*always, usually, often, sometimes, never*)	His computer **usually** doesn't work. He is **always** tired.
NOTE: Adverbs of frequency usually go before the main verb but after the verb **be**.	

(continued on next page)

2. Use the **present progressive** to tell about something that is happening right now.	Martin **is sitting** on the beach. He **isn't reading** e-mail.

3. Use the **simple present** with **non-action verbs**. Non-action verbs describe states or situations, not actions.
They can:
    a. show emotions (*hate, like, love, want, wish*)
    b. show mental states (*know, believe, remember, forget*)
    c. show possession (*have, own, belong*)
    d. describe senses (*hear, see*)
 	
NOTE: Some verbs that describe senses have an action and a non-action meaning. (*smell, taste, feel, look, think*)
	Martin **wants** a new job.
	Martin **loves** Sunny Resorts.
	He **remembers** the office as a bad dream.
	He **has** all the time he needs.
	He **sees** nothing but blue skies.
	
	Action: Martin **is looking** at an ad for Sunny Resorts. (*is looking = is reading*)
	Non-action: Martin **looks** tired. (*looks = seems / appears*)

2   *Complete the ad with the words in parentheses. Use simple present or present progressive. Read the ad with a partner.*

MARY: I just _____ springtime! Outside my window, the sun
                         (love)

                   _____, the birds _____, the flowers
                     (shine)   (sing)

                   _____ . . .
                     (bloom)

BOB: Aaachooo! [Bob sneezes]

MARY: Hey Bob, what's the matter?

BOB: It's my allergies! I _____ the spring! I
                                (hate)

                   _____ I could do something about it!
                   (wish)

ANNOUNCER: Don't let spring get you down. Try new Allerfree. One pill a day

                   _____ your allergies away. Allerfree. It really
                   (keep)

                   _____!
                   (work)

3   *Work with a partner. Look at the ads on page 13. Take turns describing what is happening in each ad. Use the simple present and present progressive and the verbs provided.*

Example

STUDENT A: The mother is holding the baby.
STUDENT B: She loves the baby....

hold / love / kiss / smile / seem

stand / talk / help / look / wait

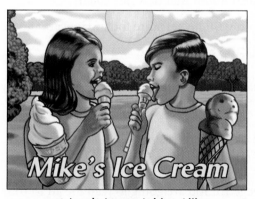

eat / melt / taste / shine / like

run / listen / look / want / look at

C SPEAKING

PRONUNCIATION: Highlighting

In radio ads, the actors emphasize, or highlight, certain words to help us focus on important information. The same pattern occurs in all kinds of communication. When we speak, we emphasize certain words to make our meaning clear.

CD 1
9 Listen to the ad. Notice how the capitalized words sound.

LIZ: Hi, Kathy ... Say ... did you do something to your hair?
KATHY: Yup! I colored it with **YOUNGER YOU**.
LIZ: It's **AMAZING**! You really **DO** look younger!
KATHY: **THANKS! NOW** people don't believe I'm a **GRANDMOTHER**.
LIZ: **I** should try it.
KATHY: It's so **EASY** to **USE**. Just **MIX** it with your shampoo, **WASH**, and **RINSE**.
LIZ: Sounds **GREAT**!
ANNOUNCER: Only five minutes to a **YOUNGER** you.

To highlight, or emphasize, a word in a sentence, use strong stress.

- Say the word with a higher pitch (tone).
- Say the word louder.
- Make the word longer.

1 *Read the conversations. Circle the words that you think will be highlighted.*

1. KATHY: Hello?

   LIZ: Kathy! I took your advice.

   KATHY: What advice?

   LIZ: I colored my hair.

   KATHY: With Younger You?

   LIZ: Yes! It's great!

2. KATHY: Did you hear about that new flea collar?

   LIZ: Yes, I'm going to the pet store today. How about you?

   KATHY: I think I'll stop by tomorrow.

CD 7
10 *Listen to the conversations and check your answers. Compare your answers with a partner's.*

2 *Work with a partner to complete the activity.*

Student A

1. Look at Ad 1 on page 15. You are going to read the ad to your partner two times. Circle the important information that you will highlight. Highlight the words you have circled by saying them louder, longer, and/or with a high pitch and strong stress.

2. Listen as Student B reads Ad 2 on page 15. Circle the words that your partner highlights.

Student B

1. Listen as Student A reads Ad 1. Circle the words that your partner highlights.

2. Look at Ad 2. You are going to read the ad to your partner two times. Circle the important information that you will highlight. Highlight the words you have circled by saying them louder, longer, and/or with a high pitch and strong stress.

When you are finished, compare your answers. Did you circle the same words? Discuss any differences.

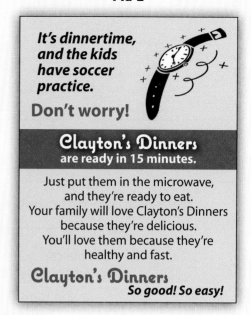

Now find another partner and repeat the exercise. This time switch ads. (Student A reads Ad 2. Student B reads Ad 1.)

◀ FUNCTION: Attention Grabbers

Attention grabbers are techniques that you can use to get a listener's attention. These techniques are often used in advertising. They are also used to get an audience's attention at the beginning of an oral presentation.

ATTENTION GRABBERS	
1. Give a solution to a problem.	"Car theft is one of the most common crimes in the United States. Many people have experienced car theft or know someone whose car has been stolen. Luckily, there now is a solution to this problem. . . ."
2. Ask a question.	"Have you ever walked out to a parking lot and discovered that your car is gone?"

(continued on next page)

3. Tell an anecdote (short story).	"Last night I left the office at 7:00 P.M., car keys in hand, and started to look for my car. I was surprised I couldn't find it because I usually park in the same place. After a couple of minutes, the awful truth hit me: My car had been stolen!"
4. Give a dramatic fact or statistic.	"Every 26 seconds, a car is stolen in the United States."

NOTE: Techniques can be combined. For example, a question can be followed by an anecdote.

1 Read the attention grabbers for an oral presentation on advertising. Write the number of the technique from the chart above. Compare your answers with a partner's.

_____ **a.** "In 1998, advertisers in the United States spent $15.4 billion on radio advertising."

_____ **b.** "As I was listening to the radio the other day, a commercial got my attention. It had a catchy song about coffee, and before I knew what was happening, I started singing along."

_____ **c.** "If you're like I am, you probably enjoy listening to the radio but hate the ads. Well, if you start to think of the ads as entertainment, you might start to enjoy them."

_____ **d.** "Have you ever wondered how advertisers get ideas for their ads?"

2 Work in a small group. Look at the ads in Grammar on page 13. Imagine you are creating radio ads for these products. Write an attention grabber to start the ad for each product. Use a different technique for each attention grabber. Then share your attention grabbers with the class.

◀ **PRODUCTION: Creating an Advertisement**

In this unit, you listened to several advertisements. Now imagine that you are writers for a major advertising company. You must **create an ad for a new product and present it to the company**. Your presentation will include an introduction to the product and a performance of the advertisement. Try to use the vocabulary, grammar, pronunciation, and attention grabbers that you learned in the unit.*

*For Alternative Speaking Topics, see page 17.

Work in a group of three. Follow the steps.

Step 1: Plan the ad.

- Choose the product and target audience for your ad.
- Decide on the appeal you will use and how you will get the consumers' attention.
- Discuss other techniques you can use in the ad (music, catchy slogan, sound effects, funny voices).

Step 2: Write a script and practice the ad.

- Make sure that each group member has a speaking part and a copy of the script.
- Keep the ad short (about 60 seconds).
- Include an attention grabber.

Step 3: Present the ad to the class. Give a brief introduction about the product and target audience. Then perform the ad.

Listening Activity

As you listen to the presentations, take notes on the questions.

1. What attention grabber is this ad using?

2. What emotional appeal is this ad using?

3. What other techniques do you observe?

4. On a scale of 1 to 5, how effective is this ad? Be prepared to explain your rating. (1 = not effective; 2 = somewhat effective; 3 = effective; 4 = very effective; 5 = extremely effective)

ALTERNATIVE SPEAKING TOPICS

Discuss one of the topics. Use the vocabulary and grammar from the unit.

1. There are many unusual places to advertise aside from TV, radio, and magazines. For example, one company covered the wall of a train station in Tokyo with pictures of its product. People could peel the pictures off the wall and take them home. Make a list of unusual methods of advertising that you have seen. Which is the most unusual? Why are advertisers doing this?

2. Children are a big target audience for advertisers. Companies hope that if they start selling products to children at an early age, children will continue to buy the products when they are adults. Some people are against advertising to children. They say that children should not be targets because they are too easily affected by advertising. What is your opinion? Should advertisers be allowed to advertise to children? Why or why not?

RESEARCH TOPICS, see page 192.

UNIT 2 Identity Theft

1 FOCUS ON THE TOPIC

A PREDICT

Discuss the questions with the class.

1. Look at the photo. What is happening to the woman's picture? Why?
2. Read the title of the unit. What is identity theft?

B. SHARE INFORMATION

Work in a small group. Read the information and discuss the questions.

Identity theft is a type of fraud. Fraud is a crime in which the criminal, or thief, lies to someone in order to get money or goods. The thieves steal personal information—such as a person's name, address, driver's license, or passport number—and use it to open bank or credit card accounts in the name of the victim, the person harmed. Victims often find out about the theft when they start getting bills for things they didn't buy.

1. What are some ways thieves can steal personal information?
2. How can you keep your personal information safe?
3. How are victims affected by identity theft?

C. BACKGROUND AND VOCABULARY

1 CD 7 🔟 *Thieves can use the Internet in many ways to steal people's identities. Read and listen to the magazine article about "phishing."*

Identity Theft Online:
Phishing

A few months ago, Henry Park received an e-mail message from his bank. The message said there was a problem with his account. It said to follow a link[1] to the bank's website. He went to a web page that asked him to **confirm** the information about his bank account by entering his bank card number and password. "I followed the instructions and got a message that everything was fine, so I forgot about it," Mr. Park said.

A few weeks later, Mr. Park received a credit card bill for almost $10,000. There were **charges** from a **department store** for a flat screen TV and a diamond ring. However, Mr. Park hadn't made any of these **purchases** and had never **authorized** anyone to use his credit card.

Mr. Park immediately called the bank to **file a complaint**. Then he found out that he was the victim of the fastest-growing type of online fraud: phishing (pronounced "fishing").

[1] **link:** a word in an Internet web page or e-mail message that takes you to another web page

How does phishing work?

Criminals pretend to work for real companies. They send e-mail messages to thousands of people. They trick people into going to a fraudulent website (which looks like a real site) and giving out their personal information. Then the thieves use the information to commit identity theft. In Mr. Park's case, the thief used the information to open a credit card in Mr. Park's name.

The experience has made Mr. Park more aware of the dangers of phishing. "I feel **exposed** now, like someone will do this to me again. And I'm more **paranoid**. I don't trust e-mail anymore."

Keep yourself safe from phishing

- Be careful about e-mail messages and websites that ask for personal information. Don't give out information that a thief could use as **proof of identification**, such as a driver's license or passport number.
- If you think you have been a victim of phishing, **deal with** it right away by calling your bank and the police. Don't wait until you start getting bills.

2 *Match the words on the left with the definitions on the right.*

_____ 1. confirm

_____ 2. charges

_____ 3. department store

_____ 4. purchases

_____ 5. authorize

_____ 6. file a complaint

_____ 7. exposed

_____ 8. paranoid

_____ 9. proof of identification

_____ 10. deal with

a. believing that you cannot trust other people

b. the amount on a bill you have to pay for something

c. documents, or papers, that show who you are

d. in danger of being harmed

e. to say or prove that something is true

f. things that have been bought

g. to do what is necessary to solve a problem

h. to give permission for something

i. a large store that sells many products

j. to send a letter saying that something bad or illegal happened

2 FOCUS ON LISTENING

A LISTENING ONE: Lily's Story

Lily's wallet was stolen at a restaurant. The thief used her personal information to open credit cards in her name. In this audio story, Lily describes what happened next.

CD 1
⑫ *Listen to the excerpt from Lily's story. Circle the correct answer. Then explain your answer.*

This is an excerpt from _____ of the story.

    a. the beginning
    b. the middle
    c. the end

◖ LISTEN FOR MAIN IDEAS

CD 1
⑬ *Listen to the whole story. Circle the correct answers.*

1. How did Lily find out that her identity had been stolen?
     a. A store called her.
     b. She got a bill in the mail.
     c. The police came to her house.

2. What happened after Lily found out about the identity theft?
     a. She got bills for purchases that she didn't make.
     b. She got phone calls from a lot of different stores.
     c. She got a letter from the police.

3. How did Lily deal with the bills she received?
     a. She went to the stores and complained to the manager.
     b. She wrote letters to the stores and explained what happened.
     c. She sent the bills back to the stores without paying them.

4. How did being a victim of identity theft affect Lily?
     a. She had to borrow money to pay the bills.
     b. She doesn't use credit cards anymore.
     c. She worries that it will happen again.

◖ LISTEN FOR DETAILS

CD 1
⑭ *Listen again. Complete the summary of Lily's story by circling the correct words or phrases.*

Lily got a phone call from a (**1.**) *jewelry / department* store saying that someone with her name had purchased a (**2.**) *television / diamond ring*. They wanted her to authorize the purchase. Lily knew there was something wrong because she was at (**3.**) *home / work* all day. The woman on the phone said that Lily was probably a victim of identity theft. She told Lily to (**4.**) *file a complaint / go to the police station.*

In the next week, Lily received almost (**5.**) *four / forty* bills from different stores, totaling about (**6.**) *thirteen / thirty* thousand dollars in charges. She was worried because the thief knew her (**7.**) *name and address / bank account number*. She didn't know what to do.

To deal with the problem, she sent (**8.**) *the police report / her proof of identification* to all the stores and explained what happened. She stopped getting new bills after about (**9.**) *four / eight* months.

Lily worries about becoming a victim again. She thinks that (**10.**) *getting a credit card / making purchases* at most department stores is too easy. The stores (**11.**) *always check / don't ask* for proof of identification. She thinks everyone should be worried about identity theft.

◖ MAKE INFERENCES

Statements can have different meanings depending on whether the intonation is rising or falling. Listen to excerpts from Lily's story and mark the rising and falling intonations. Then choose the answer that best describes what Lily means.

_{C D 1}
⑮ Excerpt One

1. Five thousand dollars! A diamond ring!

Implied Meaning

ⓐ I can't believe this.
b. I'm very angry.
c. I'm really excited.

2. OK?

a. Is that right?
b. Is that OK with you?
c. I'm right about this.

_{C D 1}
⑯ Excerpt Two

1. What are you talking about?

a. I didn't hear you.
b. Please explain what you said.
c. That doesn't make any sense.

2. A victim of what?

a. I don't understand.
b. I know you're wrong.
c. I don't agree with you.

Excerpt Three   **Implied Meaning**

a. I can't hear you.

1. Excuse me?   **b.** I don't believe what I'm hearing.

c. I'm sorry to be rude.

a. I'm confused.

2. Oh, boy.   **b.** I'm excited.

c. This is really bad.

◀ **EXPRESS OPINIONS**

For each statement, circle a number from one to five to express your opinion.
Be prepared to explain your opinions.

	Strongly Agree				Strongly Disagree
1. The stores helped Lily deal with the identity theft.	1	2	3	4	5
2. Lily's life was changed by her experience.	1	2	3	4	5
3. I feel more paranoid about identity theft after hearing Lily's story.	1	2	3	4	5

B **LISTENING TWO: Public Service Announcements**

Public service announcements (PSAs) are short presentations that give people helpful information. You often hear them on the radio or on TV.

CD 1
18 *Listen to two PSAs about how to protect yourself from identity theft. Listen and check (✓) the suggestions that you hear.*

_____ **1.** Get a locked mailbox.

_____ **2.** Be careful about giving out personal information.

_____ **3.** Check your bank and credit card statements every month.

_____ **4.** Shred (cut up) important papers before throwing them away.

_____ **5.** Leave your identification at home if you don't need it.

C INTEGRATE LISTENINGS ONE AND TWO

◖STEP 1: Organize

Complete the chart with information from Listenings One and Two.

	LILY'S STORY	PSAs
1. How do identity thieves steal personal information?	Thieves steal your wallet and take your ID.	
2. What do they do with the personal information?		
3. What should we do if we become victims of identity theft?		
4. How can we prevent identity theft?		

◖STEP 2: Synthesize

Work with a partner. Student A, you are a news reporter who wants to learn about identity theft. You are interviewing a police officer. Ask the questions. Student B, you are a police officer. Answer the reporter's questions using the information from Step 1.

a. How can identity thieves steal personal information?

b. What do they do with the information?

c. What should a person do if he or she is a victim of identity theft?

d. How can a person prevent identity theft?

Switch roles and repeat the conversation. To challenge yourselves, try doing it without looking at the chart.

3 FOCUS ON SPEAKING

A VOCABULARY

REVIEW

A word can have a meaning that is positive (good), negative (bad), or neutral (neither good nor bad). This is called the connotation of a word or expression. For example:

Positive	Negative	Neutral
safe	dangerous	department store

Work with a partner. Put the words into their correct places in the chart.

authorize	deal with	paranoid	shocking
bill	exposed	proof of identification	shred
charges	file a complaint	protect	steal
confirm	identity theft	purchase	victim
credit card	mailbox	receipt	

POSITIVE	NEGATIVE	NEUTRAL

Compare your chart with another pair's. Discuss the reasons for your choices.

1 *Read the e-mails from Lucia to her friend Shuli.*

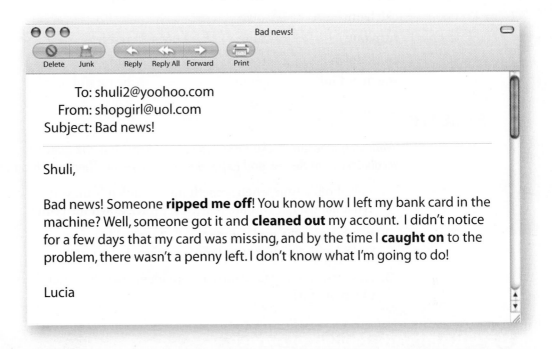

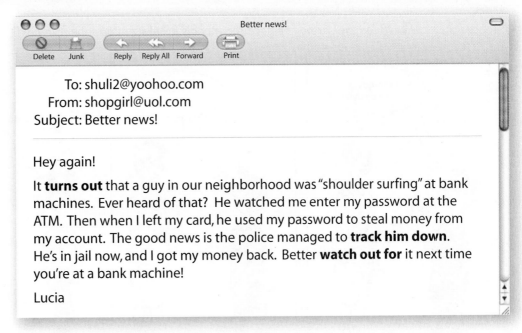

2 *Circle the correct synonym or definition for each phrasal verb.*

rip off	steal	keep
clean out	steal everything	pay
catch on	solve	realize
turn out	cause	result
track down	lose	find
watch out for	ignore	be careful of

◀ CREATE

Work with a partner. Take turns asking and answering the questions. Use the vocabulary from Review and Expand in your answers. Then switch partners and repeat.

1. Talk about a time when something was stolen from you or someone you know. What happened? Did the police ever track down the criminal?

2. What can credit card companies do to stop identity theft? Do they do enough to deal with the problem? What can they do better?

3. How can you protect yourself from identity theft? What sorts of things can you watch out for?

B **GRAMMAR: Modals of Advice**

1 *Read the cartoon. Notice the modals of advice that appear in bold.*

MODALS OF ADVICE

1. Use **should** to ask for advice.	**Should** I show them proof of identification? What **should** I do if someone steals my passport?
2. Use **should, should not,** and **ought to** to give advice. **NOTE: Ought to** is generally not used with a negative in American English.	You **should** get a locked mailbox. You **shouldn't** send personal information by e-mail. You **ought to** ask your boss to keep your personal information in a locked file.
3. Use **had better ('d better)** and **had better not ('d better not)** to give strong advice. **NOTE:** The verb that follows **should, ought to,** and **had better** always takes the base form.	You**'d better** shred those papers. You**'d better not** throw those papers in the trash.

2 *Complete each sentence with the correct modal of advice.*

1. Nasir wants to throw away some old bank statements. He _____ shred them.
   a. should **b.** ought **c.** better

2. Mira's mail got stolen. She _____ better buy a locked mailbox.
   a. should **b.** ought **c.** had

3. Someone called Azim and asked for a donation. He _____ give out his credit card number over the phone.
   a. should **b.** shouldn't **c.** better not

4. Lily got a bill for charges she didn't make. She _____ to file a complaint.
   a. ought **b.** should **c.** had better

5. Misako got an e-mail asking for her credit card account number. She _____ not send the information.
   a. shouldn't **b.** had better **c.** hadn't better

6. Chong Li gets money from a bank machine. He _____ make sure nobody is watching him.
   a. should **b.** ought not **c.** ought

7. The clerk asked Nicola to write her driver's license number on a check. She _____ not write the number on the check.
   a. better **b.** should **c.** ought to

8. Barak got a passport. He _____ lose it.
   a. ought **b.** should **c.** had better not

3 *Work in a group of three. Take turns asking for and giving advice.*

Example

STUDENT A: I haven't received any mail for three days. What **should** I do?
STUDENT B: You **should** check with the post office to see if someone is stealing your mail.
STUDENT C: If someone is stealing your mail, you **ought to** contact the police. . . .

1. I saw someone take a letter out of my neighbor's mailbox.

2. I get phone calls every day from a man I don't know. He's trying to sell me magazines.

3. Someone took some files from my office. They had personal information in them.

4. I usually have five credit cards in my wallet, but right now I seem to be missing one.

5. I have to mail my passport to Madrid to get a visa.

6. An online store sent me an e-mail asking for my credit card number.

C SPEAKING

◀ **PRONUNCIATION:** Recognizing Compounds

Compounds are two nouns used together to name one thing, for example, *mailbox*. In *mailbox* the two nouns are written together as one word. These compounds are easy to recognize. Other compounds, like *identify theft* and *credit card*, are written as two words. Compounds have a special pattern of stress and pitch.

CD 1
🔘19 Listen to the compounds and repeat them.

1. post office

2. credit card

3. identity theft

4. garbage can

5. mailbox

6. police station

7. bank account

8. roommate

The first word has the heaviest stress and high pitch.
The second word is not stressed as much and has low pitch.

post office   **credit** card

Sometimes another noun follows a compound, making a three word compound: *identity theft victim*. The first word has the heaviest stress and high pitch. The following words have less stress and lower pitch:

identity theft victim

1 *Listen to the expressions and repeat them. Circle the expressions that are pronounced as compounds, with heavy stress and high pitch on the first word. Compare your answers with a partner's.*

1. diamond ring
2. charge accounts
3. online
4. e-mail
5. Internet
6. police report
7. five thousand dollars
8. ID
9. website
10. personal information
11. 10-dollar bill
12. mailbox key

2 *Work with a partner to answer the questions. Pronounce compounds correctly.*

1. What's in your wallet?
2. What would you do if you lost your wallet or someone stole it? Has this ever happened to you?

◖ FUNCTION: Keeping a Conversation Going

To keep a conversation going both speakers need to *show that they are listening* and sometimes *encourage the other person to keep talking.*

1 *Listen to and read the example conversation. Underline the words and sounds that help to keep the conversation going. Notice the rising or falling intonation for each expression.*

A: So, I got a call from this guy. . . .

B: Uh-huh.

A: And he wanted me to give money to some organization called Amazon Rainforest something or other. You know what I'm talking about?

B: Yes, go on.

A: Anyway, I got this weird feeling from him. . . . Basically, I didn't trust him.

B: So . . . what did you do?

A: Well, I just hung up on him. You'd better be careful about these things, right?

B: Right.

KEEPING A CONVERSATION GOING	
To Show You are Listening	**To Encourage the Speaker to Keep Talking**
Yeah . . . *(rising)*	Yes. Go on. *(rising)*
Uh-huh . . . *(rising)*	And? *(rising)*
OK . . . *(rising)*	So? *(rising)*
Right. *(falling)*	And then what? *(falling)*
Wow! *(falling)*	So what . . . [did s/he say / did you do / happened next]? *(falling)*

2 *Work with a partner to complete the conversations. Choose language to show you are listening or to encourage the speaker. Make sure the language for B fits the responses for A. Then practice reading the conversations aloud with your partner.*

Conversation 1

A: So I was in my apartment and saw this man outside looking through my garbage.

B: _____

A: Well, at first I thought it was someone from our building, but then I realized I didn't recognize him.

B: _____

A: So I asked my roommate to go outside with me. Better not to go alone, right?

B: _____

A: So we went up to the guy, and I said, "Are you looking for something?"

B: _____

A: And he got really scared, dropped some papers he was holding, and ran. So I quickly grabbed the papers . . .

B: _____

A: And they were my bank statements.

Conversation 2

A: Remember that apartment I tried to rent?

B: _____

A: Well, the owner tried to rip me off. He took information from my application form and opened a credit card in my name!

B: _____! How did you find out?

A: I started getting all these bills for charges on an account that I didn't open.

B: _____

A: And then I remembered John Day was the last person I'd given my personal information to.

B: _____

A: So I went online and tracked him down. It turns out he went to jail two years ago for identity theft. . . .

◀ **PRODUCTION: Role Play**

> In this activity, you will **create and perform a 3–5-minute role play about identity theft**. A role play is a short performance. The actors take on roles, or become characters, and act out a situation. Often the situations are similar to experiences that people might have in real life. Try to use the vocabulary, grammar, pronunciation, and language for keeping a conversation going that you learned in the unit.*

Work in a group of three. Follow the steps.

Step 1: Choose a situation for the role play. Choose from the following ideas:
- filing a police report
- getting a call from a department store about a bill
- calling a credit card company about a theft
- giving advice to a friend about identity theft
- (your own idea)

Decide on the place, characters, and story. Choose from the following ideas:

Place:
- at a police station
- in a department store
- on the phone
- (your own idea)

---

*For Alternative Speaking Topics, see page 34.

Characters (think about age, personality, and feelings about the situation):

- identity theft victim
- police officer
- store employee
- identity thief
- (your own idea)

Story:

- Background: What happened before the role play starts?
- Plot: What happens during the role play?

Step 2: Create the role play. Act like your character and speak naturally. Practice the role play several times.

Step 3: Perform your role play for the class.

Listening Activity

Watch the role plays. Which role play did you like best? Discuss with a partner why you liked that role play.

ALTERNATIVE SPEAKING TOPICS

Discuss one of the topics. Use the vocabulary and grammar from the unit.

1. Tell a story about identity theft. It can be from your own experience, or something you heard or read about. Who were the victims? How did the thieves steal their identity? What happened after the theft?

2. More and more criminals are stealing personal information from computers or over the Internet. How can people protect themselves from this kind of crime?

RESEARCH TOPICS, see page 192.

Endurance Test

①FOCUS ON THE TOPIC

Ⓐ PREDICT

Discuss the questions with the class.

1. Look at the photo. Where is this man? What is this sport?

2. Read the title of the unit. *Endurance* is the ability to live with pain and suffering for a long time. What do you think the unit will be about?

rock climbing   skydiving   skateboarding

Work in a small group. Extreme sports are sports that involve height, speed, strength, or danger. Look at the photos of extreme sports and discuss the questions.

1. Which of the above sports do you think is the most dangerous? Why?

2. Why do you think people enjoy doing these sports? What do they like about them?

3. Would you like to try one of these extreme sports? Why or why not?

C **BACKGROUND** AND **VOCABULARY**

1 🔊 *Read and listen to the article about ultramarathons.*

EXTREME RUNNING ULTRAMARATHONS

A **marathon** is a running race with a 26-mile (42-kilometer) **course**. An ultramarathon is a race longer than 26 miles, often 50 to 100 miles (80.5 to 161 kilometers). There are two **formats** for ultramarathons: Some races have several short **stages** with breaks overnight. Other races go all day and night, with no stops until the runners finish.

The Race Course
Ultramarathons take place all over the world, through many types of **terrain**. There are races through rainforests, from one city to another, over mountains and rivers, or across dry desert **sand**. Every ultramarathon is **unique** because each course is different.

The *Marathon des Sables* is an ultramarathon that takes place in the Sahara Desert in Morocco. The runners race across the desert, where temperatures go up to 125°F (52°C) during the day and drop to 38°F (3°C) at night.

Racing Overnight

Many ultramarathons take several days to finish. Runners must eat and sleep on the course. In some races, food and supplies are carried in a car and the runners sleep in hotels. In other races, runners carry everything they need in backpacks and they sleep outside in **tents**.

Running Safely

To stay healthy during an ultramarathon, runners must follow safety rules. For example, runners must drink their daily **ration** of water, even if they don't feel thirsty.

Crossing the Finish Line

What is in it for the runners?[1] Many runners say they **get into** ultramarathons because they feel that normal marathons are not challenging enough. They enjoy the **experience** of crossing the finish line and completing an extremely difficult event.

_____

[1] **"What is in it for the runners":** "What are the advantages for the runners to run in the ultramarathons?"

2 *Match the words on the left with the definitions on the right.*

_____ 1. marathon

_____ 2. course

_____ 3. format

_____ 4. stage

_____ 5. terrain

_____ 6. sand

_____ 7. unique

_____ 8. tent

_____ 9. ration

_____ 10. get into

_____ 11. experience

a. being the only one of its kind

b. a piece of cloth supported by poles and rope that is used for sleeping outside

c. a specific amount of something that you are allowed to have

d. a step in a longer process

e. a type of land

f. become interested in

g. a 26-mile race

h. very small grains of rock found in a desert or beach

i. something that happens to you that affects the way you think or feel

j. the path of a race

k. the way the parts of something are arranged

2 FOCUS ON LISTENING

A LISTENING ONE: Ultrarunner Jay Batchen

CD 1 / 23 *Listen to the excerpt from an interview with runner Jay Batchen about his experience running in the Marathon des Sables. Why do you think Jay Batchen runs in the Marathon des Sables? Complete the sentence.*

He runs in the marathon because _____

_____

◀ LISTEN FOR MAIN IDEAS

CD 1 / 24 *Listen to the whole interview. All of the statements contain some **FALSE** information. Cross out the parts that are untrue and write corrections. Some statements can be corrected in more than one way.*

Example

               an endurance runner   Tim Borquin

Jay Batchen is ~~a sports reporter.~~   OR   ~~Jay Batchen~~ is a sports reporter.

1. Jay Batchen ran in the Marathon des Sables for the first time in 1999.

2. During the 1999 race, Jay became engaged to his wife.

3. The Marathon des Sables has one stage.

4. Runners have to carry water with them.

5. Runners sleep outside under the stars.

6. Jay feels that the race was a terrible experience.

◀ LISTEN FOR DETAILS

CD 1 / 25 *Listen again. Circle the best answer to complete each statement.*

1. In 1999, Jay Batchen was _____ for a TV station called the Discovery Channel.
   a. doing research about the race
   b. filming the race
   c. reporting on the race

2. Jay's future wife, Lisa, _____ the race in 1999.

    a. watched
    b. didn't finish
    c. won

3. The race course _____ every year, but it is always about 150 miles long.

    a. changes
    b. gets more difficult
    c. moves to a new place

4. The first three stages are all about _____ long.

    a. 10 miles
    b. 20 miles
    c. 26 miles

5. The fourth stage is _____.

    a. 20 miles
    b. 50 miles
    c. a full marathon

6. The fifth stage is _____.

    a. 20 miles long
    b. 50 miles long
    c. a full marathon

7. Runners get _____ at checkpoints every few miles.

    a. a serving of food
    b. a ration of water
    c. medical help

8. Runners sleep in tents that are _____.

    a. small and light
    b. crowded and uncomfortable
    c. warm and quiet

9. Jay Batchen says that he experienced _____ during the race.

    a. heat, cold, and sandstorms
    b. hunger and thirst
    c. injuries to his feet

10. Jay Batchen calls the race a "life experience" because _____.

    a. he almost didn't finish the race
    b. he shared the experience with other runners
    c. he ran faster than the other runners

◖ MAKE INFERENCES

Listen to excerpts from the interview and answer the questions.

CD 7
26 Excerpt One

What does the interviewer mean when he says, "OK, so you ended up marrying the winner of the race that you were filming"?

    a. I think that you met your wife in an unusual way.

    b. I don't believe that is how you met your wife.

    c. I am confused about how you met your wife.

CD 7
27 Excerpt Two

What does the interviewer mean when he says, "If you're able to stay standing at that point, I guess"?

    a. Can you stand up by the end of the race?

    b. You must be really tired by the end of the race.

    c. I doubt that most people can stand up at the end of the race.

CD 7
28 Excerpt Three

What does the interviewer mean when he says, "Well, you know Jay, it doesn't sound like a whole lot of fun . . . "?

    a. Most people say they didn't have fun.

    b. I understand why you enjoyed the race.

    c. It seems like it was a very difficult experience.

◖ EXPRESS OPINIONS

Discuss the questions in a small group.

    1. What's your opinion of Jay Batchen and the other runners in the Marathon des Sables? Do you admire them or do you think they are crazy? Explain.

    2. What do you think is more important in an endurance race: physical strength or emotional strength? Or are they equally important? Explain.

Ⓑ LISTENING TWO: Sports Psychology

CD 7
29 *Listen to an excerpt from a lecture in a sports psychology class about the motivation of endurance athletes. Circle the best answer to complete each statement.*

    1. Endurance athletes are often _____.
      a. very healthy
      b. high achievers
      c. professional athletes

2. They focus on achieving personal goals, not _____.
   a. finishing the event
   b. supporting other athletes
   c. winning the race

3. They choose goals that _____.
   a. are easy to achieve
   b. they have achieved before
   c. are a difficult challenge

4. They usually feel the other athletes are _____.
   a. friends who they can talk to
   b. opponents they want to beat
   c. partners in the experience

5. Endurance athletes are also motivated by _____.
   a. the strong emotions they feel while racing
   b. the prizes they win at the end of a race
   c. the exercise they get while racing

C INTEGRATE LISTENINGS ONE AND TWO

STEP 1: Organize

Answer the questions. Provide general information from the lecture and examples from the interview with Jay Batchen.

	GENERAL INFORMATION (FROM THE LECTURE)	SPECIFIC EXAMPLES (FROM THE INTERVIEW)
1. What is an ultramarathon?	a long running race with extreme conditions	• a 154-mile stage race • in the Sahara Desert • hot days, cold nights, and sandstorms
2. How do endurance athletes feel about winning their races?		
3. How do endurance athletes feel about their opponents in the race?		
4. Why do athletes run in endurance races?		

STEP 2: Synthesize

Work with a partner. Student A, you are a sports reporter interviewing an endurance athlete about running in the Marathon des Sables. Ask the questions. Student B, you are an endurance athlete. Answer the reporter's questions using the information from Step 1.

1. What is the Marathon des Sables?

2. You didn't win the race or even come close to winning. How do you feel about that?

3. How do you feel about your opponents in the race? Did you get upset when other runners passed you?

4. There are a lot of races that are shorter and easier than this one. Why do you run endurance races rather than easier races?

Switch roles and repeat the conversation. For an added challenge, try to do it without looking at the chart.

3 FOCUS ON SPEAKING

◀ REVIEW

Complete the crossword puzzle on the next page with the words from the box. Two words are NOT used.

achieve	experience	motivation
athletes	finish line	opponent
challenge	get into	sand
course	goal	stage
endurance	marathon	terrain
		unique

Across

1. My _____ is to compete in three races this year, but I don't know if I'll have time.

3. Jay Batchen had an important life _____ running in the Marathon des Sables.

5. We finished the first _____ of the race today, and the second one is tomorrow.

7. The New York City _____ is the largest running race in the world.

9. The runners were tired when they finally crossed the _____ _____.

10. Many athletes _____ _____ endurance sports because they want a challenge.

11. There were 100 _____ running in the race.

12. The race _____ is the same length every year.

13. This is a _____ race. No other race is like it.

14. _____ athletes run in long, difficult races.

Down

2. My _____ ran faster, so he won the race.

4. The runners enjoyed the _____ of doing something difficult.

6. My _____ for doing sports is to stay healthy and have fun.

8. I hope to _____ my goal of finishing the race.

1 ᴄᴅ ⁊ *Read and listen to the conversation. Then practice reading the conversation with a partner.*

REPORTER: How's it going out there?

ATHLETE: I'm OK, but it was a tough day. I fell down about halfway, and that really **(1) threw me for a loop**. I never felt the same after that.

REPORTER: How come?

ATHLETE: Well, sometimes I can **(2) be my own worst enemy**. I mean, I start thinking negative thoughts, and I don't run well.

REPORTER: How did you keep yourself going after that?

ATHLETE: I **(3) set my heart on** finishing this race. I really want it. I got a good start, and I don't want to **(4) blow my chance**.

REPORTER: So, after your problems today, what's your plan for tomorrow?

ATHLETE: Well, I want to enjoy myself more.

REPORTER: **(5) Easier said than done**!

ATHLETE: So true! But I know **(6) I have what it takes** to finish this race, so I just need to go out and try my best.

2 *Match the phrases in the conversation with their meanings. Write the number of each phrase in the correct blank.*

_____ **a.** decided that I really want to do this

_____ **b.** miss my opportunity by making a mistake

_____ **c.** I have the ability to be successful.

_____ **d.** surprised and confused me

_____ **e.** behave in a way that causes problems later

_____ **f.** That's really difficult to do.

◖ CREATE

1 *Think about an important goal you have in your life. It can be a goal in sports, school, work, or other areas. Consider the examples.*

- Learn English
- Become a doctor
- Run in a marathon
- Buy a house
- Travel around the world

2 *Work with a partner. Take turns asking and answering questions about your goal. Use the words and phrases from the box in your answers.*

1. What is your goal? When did you first set your heart on this goal?

2. When do you think you will achieve the goal? What stage are you at in the process (beginning, middle, end)?

3. How is your experience so far? Do you enjoy it?

4. What challenges make it difficult to achieve the goal? Are you ever your own worst enemy? Has anything thrown you for a loop? Please explain.

5. What is your motivation for achieving the goal?

6. Why do you think you have what it takes to achieve the goal? Is there something unique about you that will help you achieve it?

blow my chance	endurance	get into
easier said than done	format	opponent

Example

STUDENT A: What is your goal?
STUDENT B: I want to be a newspaper reporter.
STUDENT A: When did you first set your heart on this goal?
STUDENT B: I first got into reporting when I was in high school. I started working on the school newspaper.

B GRAMMAR: Reflexive and Reciprocal Pronouns

1 *Read the excerpt from an article about motivation. The words in bold are reflexive and reciprocal pronouns. Draw an arrow from these pronouns to the words they refer to.*

What motivates an extreme athlete like Jay Batchen to push **himself** to the limit? One thing we know is that athletes like Jay tend to be risk takers. They feel excited when they put **themselves** in risky or dangerous situations. This feeling can become stronger when athletes compete against **one another**. For example, if an extreme skier sees another skier doing a difficult jump, she might challenge **herself** to do an even more dangerous jump.

REFLEXIVE AND RECIPROCAL PRONOUNS

1. Use a **reflexive pronoun** when the subject and object of a sentence are the same person or thing. The reflexive pronouns are: **myself** **ourselves** **yourself** **yourselves** **herself** **himself** **themselves** **itself**	*Jay Batchen* pushes **himself** to the limit. *They* put **themselves** in dangerous situations.
2. Use **yourself / yourselves** in **imperative sentences** with reflexive pronouns. Use: • **yourself** when the subject is singular. • **yourselves** when the subject is plural. **NOTE:** In imperative sentences, the subject is *you,* even though it isn't stated.	(you) Believe in **yourself** and you will succeed. (you) Prepare **yourselves** for a tough race.
3. Use a **reciprocal pronoun** when the subject and object are the same people, and the people have a relationship. Use: • **each other** for two people. • **one another** for more than two people. **NOTE:** Often people use **each other** and **one another** in the same way.	*Marge and Susan* competed against **each other**. The *athletes* competed against **one another**.
4. Reciprocal pronouns and plural reflexive pronouns have different meanings.	*Marge and Susan* helped **each other**. (Marge helped Susan, and Susan helped Marge.) *Marge and Susan* helped **themselves**. (Marge helped herself and Susan helped herself.)

2 *Complete the conversation with the correct reflexive and reciprocal pronouns.*

PIERRE: This is Pierre Blanc, reporting on the Extreme Alpine Road Race in France. I'm talking to Tomas Bergetti, coach of cyclist Bridgit Jacobsen. Tomas, what does Bridgit do to prepare (**1.**) _____ for this race?

TOMAS: Well, she pushes (**2.**) _____ pretty hard. She gets up at 4:00 A.M. every day to ride, and she only takes one day off a month!

PIERRE: Wow! I know her brother Hans is on the same team. Do Bridgit and Hans help (**3.**) _____ with training?

TOMAS: Absolutely! But they both have personal goals for (**4.**) _____, so they try to focus on that, rather than competing against (**5.**) _____.

PIERRE: You must be very proud of her big win in the race today!

TOMAS: Yes, we're very happy. We're going to reward (**6.**) _____ by going out for a big dinner!

3 *Work with a partner. Guess what Bridgit and her teammates do in these situations. Choose verbs from the box and use reflexive and reciprocal pronouns in your answers. Try to think of more than one answer for each situation.*

be disappointed in	compete against	feel sorry for	push
blame	enjoy	imagine	support
challenge	feel proud of	make / force	tell

What does Bridgit do if . . .

1. she starts feeling tired at the end of a race?

Example

She imagines herself crossing the finish line.

2. she sleeps late and misses her morning training?

3. she goes to a party to celebrate winning a race?

4. she doesn't achieve her training goals?

5. her teammate wins a race?

What do Bridgit and her teammates do / feel . . .

6. when they are racing together?

7. if their team wins?

8. if their team loses?

◀ **PRONUNCIATION: Expressions with** *other*

The word *other* joins very closely to the word in front of it. In *another*, the two words (*an* and *other*) are written together. In the expression *each other*, the two words are written separately, but they are joined just as closely together.

CD 1
31 Listen to the boldfaced expressions below.

A: **The other night** I was talking to my roommate about starting a regular exercise program. She wants to start, too.

B: You should do it together. You'll motivate **each other.**

A: I have **another** motivation—the clothes in my closet that don't fit anymore!

PRONUNCIATION POINTS TO REMEMBER

1. Join *other* closely to the word before it. Pronounce the two words as if they were one word. Say "eachother."

2. Pronounce the "th" in *other* correctly—the tip of your tongue is between your teeth. Try it.

3. When *the* precedes *other*, it is pronounced /ðiy/ (like the vowel in *tree*). Use the /y/ in /ðiy/ to join to *other*. Try it: *they other*

---

1 **CD 1** **32** *Listen to the phrases and repeat them. Then choose three phrases and say them to the class. Join the words together closely and don't forget* **th.**

1. the other night (recently, at night)

2. the other day (recently)

3. something or other (an idiom for "something")

4. one another

5. each other

6. some other

7. one thing or another

8. every other day (on alternate days: Monday, Wednesday, Friday, etc.)

2 Fill in the blanks with expressions from Exercise 1. Check your answers with a partner's and then practice reading the sentences to your partner. Join words together and pronounce the **th** in **other** carefully.

1. _____ _____ _____ my two roommates and I go for a long walk.

2. _____ _____ _____ we were walking in the park behind a very old couple.

3. They were holding hands and talking to _____ _____.

4. The woman slipped on _____ _____ _____ and fell.

5. _____ _____ people were passing by, but they didn't do anything.

6. We ran to help them and when we saw them, we realized we all knew_____ _____. They live in our building.

3 Work with a partner. Create five short conversations by matching Student A's part with Student B's part. Then practice the conversations. The underlined words are idioms with **other**. Do you know what they mean?

Student A's Part

1. Sharon's sons are <u>at each other's throats</u> all the time. She doesn't know what to do.

2. This has been one of the worst days of my life.

3. What's the difference between an extreme sport and an endurance sport?

4. The lecture was really hard. I don't think I remember anything the professor said.

5. The old couple that I helped in the park last week brought me a cake.

Student B's Part

a. Nothing, as far as I'm concerned—<u>six of one, half a dozen of another</u>.

b. Me neither—the material went <u>in one ear and out the other</u>.

c. I guess it's true that <u>one good turn deserves another</u>.

d. She might not be able to do anything. My brother and I <u>fought with each other</u> until he went away to school.

e. Don't give up. <u>Tomorrow's another day</u>.

◀ FUNCTION: Asking for and Expressing Opinions

1 Read the conversation. Notice the language for asking for and expressing opinions.

SUNG LEE: Look at that guy. **What do you think** he's doing?
AHMED: **It looks like** he's running forward and then backward. Maybe he's training for a race.
ELI: **I don't think so.** See how slowly he's going? He can't be a racer.
AHMED: **You're right.** He is pretty slow. **I think** he's probably just doing that for fun.

ASKING FOR AND EXPRESSING OPINIONS

To Ask for an Opinion

Use **What do you think (about)...?** to ask for a general opinion.

Use **Do you think (that...)** / **Do you agree (with)...?** to ask about specific points.

What do you think about extreme sports?

Do you think extreme sports are dangerous?
Do you agree (with Eli) that extreme sports are dangerous?

To Express an Opinion

Use **I think** to sound stronger and more certain.

Use **I'm pretty sure** or **It seems like** to sound less certain and/or more polite.

I think Bridgit won the race.

I'm pretty sure Bridgit won the race.
It seems like Bridgit won the race.

To Agree

To agree with someone use:

    Yeah / Yes ...
    (I think) You're right.
    I agree (with name).

I think Ron is the best runner.
Yeah, he is.
I think you're right.
I agree (with Michelle).

To Disagree

To disagree with someone use:

Indirect **I don't know.**
          I'm not sure about that.
Direct   **I don't think so.**
          I disagree (with name).

Indirect disagreement sounds more polite.
Direct disagreement sounds stronger and can be less polite.

I don't know. Jack is a great runner, too.
I'm not sure about that. Jack is a great runner, too.
I don't think so. Jack is better.
I disagree (with Kyoko). Jack is better.

---

2 *Read the two conversations and discuss the differences. Which conversation is more direct, and which is more indirect and polite? Underline the words and phrases that helped you decide.*

1. **A:** I think extreme sports are the most dangerous sports.

     B: I don't think so. All sports can be dangerous.

     C: You're right. I think that athletes hurt themselves in all sports, not just extreme sports.

2. **A:** I think that extreme sports are the most dangerous sports.

     B: I'm not sure about that. It seems to me that all sports can be dangerous.

     C: Yeah. I'm pretty sure that athletes hurt themselves in all sports, not just extreme sports.

3 *Work in a group of three. Look at the pictures of the athletes. Discuss how you think each athlete is feeling. Make sure that everyone in the group gets to express an opinion. Under each picture write the adjective(s) that you think best describe(s) the athlete's feelings.*

angry

Example

ROBERTO: I think the guy on the left is angry. Look at his face. Doesn't he look angry?

KEIKO: I don't know. See how he's looking at the ball? It seems like he's trying to get it. What do you think, Maria?

MARIA: I agree with Roberto. He looks angry to me.

◖ **PRODUCTION: Small Group Discussion**

> An *aphorism* is a short, wise phrase that is easy to remember. It expresses an idea or belief in a new and interesting way. In this activity, you will ***examine and discuss some aphorisms and then write your own aphorism***. Try to use the vocabulary, grammar, pronunciation, and language for asking and expressing opinions that you learned in the unit.*

---

*For Alternative Speaking Topics, see page 52.

Work in a small group. Follow the steps.

Step 1: Read and discuss the aphorisms in the box.
- What are the athletes saying about their motivation for running? Explain.
- Which aphorism do you like best? Why?
- Which aphorism expresses an idea or feeling you have had? Explain.

Step 2: As a group, create an aphorism about motivation. Think of a situation in which a person needs motivation, such as doing sports, studying, working, practicing a musical instrument, or anything else.

Step 3: Write the aphorism on the blackboard or on a big piece of paper. As a group, share the aphorism with the class and explain its meaning.

Endurance Runners on Motivation

1. "Motivation is what gets you started. Habit is what keeps you going."
   —Jim Ryan

2. "When I run a long race, I get to meet some new people—including myself."
   —Anonymous

3. "The fear of not finishing is often greater than the fear of pain."
   —Laurie Dexter

4. "The heart controls the mind, and the mind controls the body."
   —Jim Lampley

5. "Find the joy in the journey—the finish line will come soon enough."
   —Anonymous

6. "The greatest pleasure in life is doing what people say you cannot do."
   —Bagehot

ALTERNATIVE SPEAKING TOPICS

Discuss one of the topics. Use the vocabulary and grammar from the unit.

1. In Listening Two the professor talked about two motivations for endurance sports: the satisfaction of achieving goals and the closeness between athletes. Can you think of other reasons why extreme athletes do their sports?

2. Research has shown that a large number of emergency room doctors do extreme sports. What do you think is the reason for this? Can you think of other professions that might match the personality of the extreme athlete?

RESEARCH TOPICS, see page 193.

UNIT 4
Separated by the Same Language

1 FOCUS ON THE TOPIC

A PREDICT

Discuss the questions with the class.

1. Look at the cartoon. Are the men talking about the same thing?

2. In what country do people say *queue*? In what country do they say *line*?

3. English novelist Sir Walter Besant (1836–1901) said: "England and America are two countries separated by the same language." What did he mean?

53

Complete the activity in a small group.

1. When you hear a person speak in your native language, what can you tell from that person's accent? Check (✓) one or more items.

   hometown   _____

   economic class   _____

   level of education   _____

   profession   _____

   age   _____

   intelligence   _____

   other: _____

   _____

2. Are some accents in your native language considered better than others? Why or why not?

C BACKGROUND AND VOCABULARY

1 🔘 CD 7 **33** *Read and listen to the excerpt from a linguistics textbook about dialects.*

Language and Literature   55

DIALECT

A *dialect* is a form of a language with grammar, pronunciation, and vocabulary that differ from other forms of the language. A dialect develops when a group of same-language speakers are separated in some way. *Regional dialects* develop when speakers are separated by geography such as rivers  and mountains. *Social dialects* develop when one group is separated from another socially because of differences in economic class, level of education, culture, ethnicity, or age. A *standard dialect* is a dialect that is mostly used in the media (TV, radio, and newspapers).

DIALECT CASE STUDIES

Case Study #1

"My son is very **bright**. He always does very well in school, but I worry that people won't see that because of the way he speaks. He uses a lot of the **slang** that's popular with teenagers these days. I'm afraid that people will **stereotype** him because of the way he talks. To me, he sounds uneducated and rude. He says, though, it's part of his **identity** and he would be a different person if he talked a different way. Also, he says that all his friends talk that way and he wants to **fit in** with them."

Case Study #2

"I have a Boston accent. When I lived in Boston, I never thought about it much, but I became **aware of** my accent when I moved to the West Coast. People here always **comment on** my accent and sometimes laugh when I say certain words. I don't think they are **intentionally** trying to hurt my feelings; they just don't realize that it hurts me. It makes me feel **self-conscious**, and I'm always worried about what people think of me. I want people to **accept** me the way I am."

2 *Circle the answer that correctly completes the definition of each boldfaced word.*

1. A **bright** person is _____.
   - **a.** happy
   - **b.** intelligent

2. **Slang** is _____ used by people in a particular group.
   - **a.** formal words
   - **b.** informal words

3. To **stereotype** means to have ideas about what people are like because of how they _____.
   - **a.** play sports
   - **b.** look or sound

4. A person's **identity** is _____.
   - **a.** who a person is
   - **b.** where a person lives

5. To **fit in** means to _____ others in a group.
   - **a.** be more fashionable than
   - **b.** be similar to

6. To become **aware of** something means to _____ something.
   - **a.** know about
   - **b.** stop

7. To **comment on** something means to _____ it.
   - **a.** give an opinion about
   - **b.** ignore

8. When something is done **intentionally**, it is done _____.
   - **a.** by accident
   - **b.** on purpose

9. Being **self-conscious** means being worried about what _____.
   - **a.** you think of other people
   - **b.** other people think of you

10. To **accept** someone means to feel that the person _____.
    - **a.** is good enough
    - **b.** should change

2 FOCUS ON LISTENING

A LISTENING ONE: Accent and Identity

Lisa is a graduate student in a linguistics class. She is doing a class project on how people feel about their accents. You will hear her interview Peter, a native English speaker.

🎧 CD 1
34
Listen to the excerpt. Where do you think Peter is from? Circle the name of the country.

a. United States **d.** Australia

b. England **e.** South Africa

c. St. Vincent

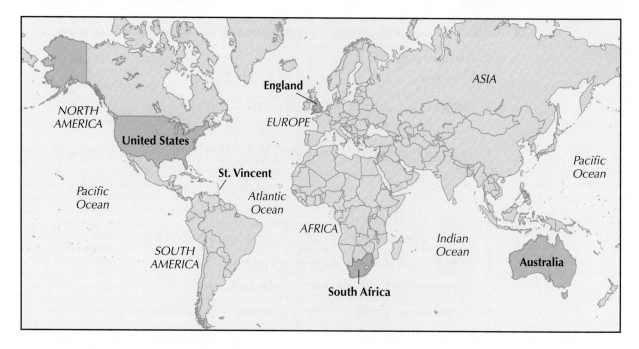

◀ LISTEN FOR MAIN IDEAS

🎧 CD 1
35
Listen to the interview between Lisa and Peter. Circle the best answer to complete each statement.

1. Before Peter came to the United States, he _____ his accent.
   a. felt self-conscious about
   b. wanted to preserve
   c. was not aware of

2. When Peter first came to the United States, he felt that he _____ because of his accent.

    a. didn't fit in
    b. couldn't communicate
    c. didn't meet people

3. Now Peter feels that his accent is _____.

    a. helpful in his work
    b. different than before
    c. part of his identity

◖ LISTEN FOR DETAILS

36 *Listen again. Circle the best answer to complete each statement.*

1. Peter grew up in _____.

    a. England   **b.** St. Vincent   **c.** Australia

2. Peter felt that some people thought he was not _____ because he talked slowly.

    a. interesting   **b.** confident   **c.** intelligent

3. Peter got tired of explaining his _____ to people he met.

    a. opinions   **b.** culture   **c.** background

4. Peter tried to change his accent so that he could fit in _____.

    a. at college   **b.** at work   **c.** at home

5. Peter liked living at International House because everyone _____.

    a. accepted him   **b.** spoke another language   **c.** helped him change his accent

6. When Peter goes home to St. Vincent, his friends say that his accent _____.

    a. sounds very American   **b.** is more difficult to understand   **c.** is exactly the same

7. Today Peter lives in _____.

    a. St. Vincent   **b.** the United States   **c.** England

8. Now Peter _____ his accent.

    a. is comfortable with   **b.** still has problems with   **c.** is trying to change

◖ MAKE INFERENCES

Listen to the excerpts about different times in Peter's life. Rate how positive or negative Peter felt during each time period. Circle a number from –2 (most negative) to +2 (most positive). Then write down some key words that show how he felt. Share your answers with the class.

		Negative				Positive

C D 7
37 Excerpt One: In St. Vincent

	Negative				Positive
How did Peter feel about his accent?	–2	–1	0	+1	+2
How did Peter feel about himself?	–2	–1	0	+1	+2

Key words: _____

C D 7
38 Excerpt Two: During college in the United States

	Negative				Positive
How did Peter feel about his accent?	–2	–1	0	+1	+2
How did Peter feel about himself?	–2	–1	0	+1	+2

Key words: _____

C D 7
39 Excerpt Three: Now, in the United States

	Negative				Positive
How does Peter feel about his accent?	–2	–1	0	+1	+2
How does Peter feel about himself?	–2	–1	0	+1	+2

Key words: _____

◖ EXPRESS OPINIONS

Discuss the questions in a small group.

1. How did Peter's feelings about his accent change? Can you understand why?

2. Do you think it is polite to ask people about their accents? Why or why not?

3. For several years, Peter felt self-conscious about his accent. Would you feel the same way? Why or why not?

4. Peter says that a person's accent is part of his or her identity. Do you agree? Explain your answer.

LISTENING TWO: Code-Switching

You will hear a lecture on code-switching. In linguistics, the word *code* is used to mean "language" or "dialect."

CD 1
40 *Listen to the lecture. Fill in the missing information in the notes.*

LINGUISTICS

Code-switching = changing _____

   - Speak one language _____

   - Another language _____

Teen dialect (slang)

Parents _____

   e.g., To friend: "Gotta bounce. We gotta

   meet the crew."

     To dad: "We have to _____.

   We're meeting our _____."

   Teens use teen dialect:

     - to _____ with friends

     - to _____ from adults

C INTEGRATE LISTENINGS ONE AND TWO

◖ **STEP 1: Organize**

*Would Peter, from St. Vincent, and a teenager from the United States agree with these statements about the way they speak? Read the statements and write **A** (agree) or **D** (disagree). Then write examples from the listenings to explain your answers.*

STATEMENT	OPINION	EXAMPLES
1. "I speak differently with different people."	Peter: _D_ Teen: _A_	Peter: Doesn't try to change his accent now. Friends say that he doesn't have an American accent. Teen: Speaks teen dialect with friends and standard dialect with parents.
2. "Some people comment on the way I speak."	Peter: _____ Teen: _____	
3. "Some people don't like the way I speak."	Peter: _____ Teen: _____	
4. "I want to change the way I speak."	Peter: _____ Teen: _____	
5. "The way I speak is part of my identity."	Peter: _____ Teen: _____	

◖ **STEP 2: Synthesize**

Work in a group of three. Imagine that Peter and a teenager are being interviewed together. One person plays the part of the interviewer and asks the questions. The other two people play Peter and a teenager and answer the questions based on the information in Step 1.

1. Do you change the way you speak in different situations, or when talking to different people? Why?

2. What do other people say about how you speak?

3. Who likes the way you speak? Who doesn't like it?

4. Do you want to change the way you speak? Why or why not?

5. In what way is your speech a part of your identity?

Switch roles and repeat the role play so that each person gets a turn playing the interviewer, Peter, and the teenager.

③ FOCUS ON SPEAKING

Ⓐ VOCABULARY

◖ REVIEW

Work with a partner. Read the quotes. Choose the words or phrases from the box to complete the summaries of the quotes.

accents	code-switches	self-conscious about
accepts	intentionally	slang
as part of his identity	obviously	standard dialect
aware of	regional dialect	~~stereotyped~~
		to fit in with friends

1. "As soon as I heard my new coworker's accent, I knew he wasn't very bright."

   The speaker _____stereotyped_____ her coworker because of his accent.

2. "It's clear that John gave me the wrong information."

   The speaker is saying that John _____ gave her the wrong information.

3. "It wasn't an accident that John gave me the wrong information."

   The speaker thinks John _____ gave her the wrong information.

4. "In the United States, we pronounce words like *class* and *water* differently than they do in England."

   The speaker is giving an example of different _____.

5. "Some teens say *Gotta bounce*, meaning "I have to go."

   The speaker is giving an example of _____.

6. "Mary Ellen sounds like she comes from the southern part of the country."

   Mary Ellen speaks a _____.

7. "Roger sounds like the reporters on TV."

   Roger speaks a _____.

8. "When I'm with my English-speaking friends, I speak English, but with my Chinese friends I speak Chinese."

   The speaker _____ with his friends.

9. "I know that I speak with an accent, but people usually understand me."

   The speaker is _____ his accent.

10. "I get embarrassed when people don't understand me because of my accent."

    The speaker is _____ her accent.

11. "I use slang because all my friends talk that way."

    The speaker uses slang _____.

12. "I use slang because it shows people who I am."

    The speaker uses slang _____.

13. "My coworker has an accent, but it doesn't bother me. He's a nice guy, so I don't care how he speaks."

    The speaker _____ his coworker the way he is.

◖ EXPAND

1 🔘 *Read and listen to the conversation between two coworkers.*

CD 7
41

ABBY: This guy at work, I think he's trying to be funny, but he keeps making fun of my accent. Whenever I'm around, he starts talking in a really bad Australian accent and saying things like, "G'day, Mate!"

MARCO: Really? That's annoying.

ABBY: I know! I want him to **lay off**, but I'm not sure how to tell him. I don't want to be rude.

MARCO: Well, don't worry about that—he's the one being rude. And if you don't like it, you have to **stick up for yourself** and make him stop.

ABBY: Yeah, but I don't want to **make a big deal about it**. I have to work with him every day, so I don't want him to be mad at me.

MARCO: Maybe, but his behavior really **crosses the line**. It's not right for him to treat you like that.

ABBY: You're right. I shouldn't **get hung up about** what he thinks. He's not considering my feelings.

MARCO: Exactly. Hey, how about talking to your boss? Ask her to **deal with it**. She can talk to him and make him stop.

ABBY: Yeah. Maybe I'll do that.

2 *Match the phrases on the left with the definitions on the right.*

____ **1.** lay off

____ **2.** stick up for yourself

____ **3.** make a big deal about it

____ **4.** cross the line

____ **5.** get hung up about

____ **6.** deal with it

a. worry too much about

b. behave in a way that is not acceptable

c. defend yourself from criticism

d. make something more important than it should be

e. stop doing something that is bad or annoying

f. take care of a problem

◀ **CREATE**

This game of Truth or Dare¹ will help you review vocabulary from the unit and learn more about your classmates.

1. Play in a small group. Use a pair of dice or pieces of paper numbered 1–12. The players take turns choosing a number.

2. After choosing a number, the player looks at the corresponding number in the chart on page 64 and decides whether to "Tell the Truth" or "Take a Dare." If you choose "Take a Dare," use vocabulary from the box below.

Cross off the word after a player uses it. Each word may be used only once.

accept	fit in with	regional dialect
aware of	get hung up about	self-conscious
code-switch	identity	slang
cross the line	intentionally	standard dialect
deal with it	lay off	stereotype
dialect	make a big deal about	stick up for yourself

───────────────

¹**dare:** to challenge someone to do something that is difficult or embarrassing

TELL THE TRUTH

Complete the task truthfully.

1. Describe something that you *get hung up about.*

2. Describe a time when someone *made a big deal about* something.

3. Describe a time you saw someone get *stereotyped* because of the way he or she spoke, looked, or acted.

4. Think of something that is an important part of your *identity* and describe why it is important.

5. Describe a time when you had to *stick up for yourself* or someone else in a difficult situation.

6. Describe a time when you had to tell someone to *lay off.*

7. Describe something you have done to *fit in with* a group of friends.

8. Describe a time you saw someone act in a way that *crossed the line.*

9. Give an example of the *slang* you use with your friends.

10. Give an example of when you *code-switch* between two dialects or languages.

11. Describe a problem you had and how you decided to *deal with it.*

12. Explain whether you have a *standard* or *regional dialect* in your native language.

TAKE A DARE

Complete the task with a word or phrase from the vocabulary box on page 63.

1. Give the definition of the word / phrase.

2. Spell the word / phrase without looking at it.

3. Spell the word / phrase backward without looking at it.

4. Say another word / phrase that has a similar meaning.

5. Say a word / phrase that has the opposite meaning of the word.

6. Use the word / phrase in a sentence about yourself.

7. Use the word / phrase in a sentence about someone else.

8. Use some of the letters in the word / phrase to spell a new word.

9. Translate the word / phrase into your native language.

10. Without speaking, act out the meaning of the word / phrase.

11. Make a question using the word / phrase.

12. Say a sentence in the past tense using the word / phrase.

1 *Read the paragraph. Underline the modals **can, can't, could,** and **couldn't.** Then discuss the questions with the class.*

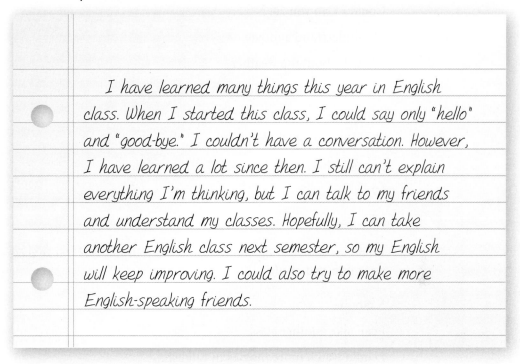

I have learned many things this year in English class. When I started this class, I could say only "hello" and "good-bye." I couldn't have a conversation. However, I have learned a lot since then. I still can't explain everything I'm thinking, but I can talk to my friends and understand my classes. Hopefully, I can take another English class next semester, so my English will keep improving. I could also try to make more English-speaking friends.

1. Which sentences in the paragraph are about past events?

2. Which are about the present?

3. Which are about the future?

MODALS OF ABILITY AND POSSIBILITY	
1. The modals **can** and **could** are followed by the base form of the verb.	I **can do** that. **Could** you **hear** me?
2. Use **can** to express ability in the present. **Can't** is the negative of *can*. Use **could** to express ability in the past. **Couldn't** is the negative of *could*.	She **can** speak English. He **can't** speak French. Last year, I **could** say a few words in English. I **couldn't** have a conversation in English last year.
3. **Can** and **could** also express possibility in the future.	Next year, you **can** study French. He **could** study more next time.

2 *Work with a partner. Discuss how much your English has improved in the past year. Using the list below, take turns asking and answering questions about what you could and couldn't do in English a year ago and what you can and can't do in English now. Then think of other things that are not on the list.*

Could / Can you . . . ?

1. understand a movie

2. talk about the weather

3. order food in a restaurant

4. discuss international politics

5. talk on the telephone

6. talk about your interests

7. _____

8. _____

3 *What can you do in the future to improve your English? Make a list of possible things using* **can** *and* **could**.

Example

I can take another class.

I could watch more movies in English.

Share your list with a partner. Report to the class any similarities.

Example

We hope we can join a conversation group.

We both thought we could take another class.

C SPEAKING

PRONUNCIATION: *Can / Can't*

It is sometimes difficult for students to hear and pronounce the difference between *can* and *can't*. When we say *can* and *can't* by themselves or in a list of words, they have the same vowel sound. But in a sentence, the vowel in *can* usually has a very different pronunciation. If you pronounce *can* with the vowel in *can't*, native speakers may think you are saying *can't*.

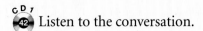

CD 7
42 Listen to the conversation.

STUDENT A: Can you speak any foreign languages?
STUDENT B: Yes, I can. I can speak Chinese. But I can't speak very fluently yet. How about you?
STUDENT A: I can read French, but I can't speak it very well.

What differences did you hear in the spoken pronunciation of *can* and *can't*?

CAN / CAN'T	
Can is not stressed in most sentences and questions. It is pronounced /kən/, with a short unclear vowel. In the sentence *They can speak Chinese*, the words *they can* rhyme with *bacon*.	They **can** /kən/ speak Chinese. They **can** /kən/ read French. They **can** /kən/ cook bacon.
Can is stressed when it ends a sentence or clause.	Yes, I **can** /kæn/. If I **can** /kæn/, I'll take a Chinese class.
Can't is always stressed. The vowel sound in *can't* is /æ/, like the vowel in *hand*.	I **can't** /kænt/ speak it very fluently yet. I **can't** /kænt/ take that Chinese class.

1 CD 7
43 *Listen to the sentences. Circle* **can** *or* **can't**. *Compare your answers with a partner's.*

1. She *can / can't* take that class.

2. He *can / can't* speak French.

3. I *can / can't* understand American slang.

4. We *can / can't* speak that dialect.

5. I *can / can't* recognize his accent.

6. She *can / can't* fit in.

7. I *can / can't* comment on that.

8. She invited me to come. I said that I *can / can't*.

2 *Work with a partner and practice pronouncing* **can** *and* **can't**. *Student A reads each sentence to Student B, using either* **can** *or* **can't**, *with the correct pronunciation. If he or she hears* **can**, *Student B says "So can /kən/ I." If he or she hears* **can't**, *Student B says "Neither can /kən/ I." After Student A completes all the sentences, switch roles. Then compare your answers with another pair's.*

1. She *can / can't* take that class.

2. He *can / can't* speak French.

3. I *can / can't* understand American slang.

4. We *can / can't* speak that dialect.

5. I *can / can't* deal with it.

6. She *can / can't* fit in.

7. I *can / can't* comment on that.

8. She invited me to come. I said that I *can / can't*.

9. I *can / can't* understand her accent.

10. She *can / can't* stick up for herself.

◖FUNCTION: Leading a Small Group Discussion

1 *Look at the pictures of a classroom discussion. What is the teacher doing in each picture? Write the letter of your answer in the blank.*

"Today I'd like to discuss . . ."

1. _____

"What do you think, Susan?"

2. _____

"Let's get back to our discussion about . . ."

3. _____

"That's all we have time for today."

4. _____

The teacher is . . .

a. beginning the discussion.

b. ending the discussion.

c. keeping the discussion on topic.

d. getting comments from different students.

In a group discussion, it is useful to have a leader to direct and control the conversation. The group leader must start and end the discussion, keep the discussion on topic, and make sure everyone has a chance to participate.

2 *Read the phrases that you can use to lead a discussion. With the class, think of other phrases that can be used in each situation and write them in the blanks.*

Starting a Discussion

- Our topic for today is . . .
- Today I'd like to discuss . . .

_____

_____

Getting Everyone to Speak

a. Asking someone to talk

- What do you think, (name)?
- (name), do you agree?

_____

_____

b. Asking someone to stop talking

- That's a good point, (name). Can we hear from someone else?
- I see your point, (name). Does anyone agree or disagree?

_____

_____

Staying on the Topic

- Let's get back to our discussion about . . .
- I'd like to return to the topic. What do you think about . . . ?

_____

_____

Ending a Discussion

- That's all we have time for today.
- So to sum up . . . (You summarize the ideas expressed in the discussion.)

_____

_____

3 *Work in a group of four. Discuss how to improve your pronunciation in English. Use the conversation guide below. One student (Leader) leads the discussion. The other three students (Students 1, 2, and 3) discuss the topic. Use ideas from the box or make up your own. Repeat the activity so that each group member plays all the parts.*

LEADER: (Start discussion) _____ the best way to improve your pronunciation when you speak English. (Ask Student 1 to talk) _____?

STUDENT 1:   I think that _____ is the best way. For me it's good because _____.

LEADER: (Ask Student 2 to talk) _____?

STUDENT 2:   I don't like _____ because _____. I think the best way to improve your pronunciation is _____. That's because _____. For example, _____.

LEADER: (Ask Student 2 to stop talking and Student 3 to talk) _____.

STUDENT 3:   I think _____ because _____.

LEADER: (End discussion) _____.

Pronunciation Activities

listen to pronunciation tapes

practice in a language lab

watch TV or movies

live with a family or roommate that speaks English

take pronunciation classes

travel or live in an English-speaking country

make friends with native speakers

listen to the radio

learn songs

Other: _____

◖ **PRODUCTION: Leading a Small Group Discussion**

In this activity, you will each *lead a small group discussion related to language*. Try to use the vocabulary, grammar, pronunciation, and discussion-leading skills that you learned in the unit.*

---

*For Alternative Speaking Topics, see page 72.

Work in a group of four. Follow the steps.

Step 1: Each student chooses a different situation from the list.

Situation 1

Mike is a TV news reporter from the state of Mississippi. He is applying for a job as a reporter on a national news program that will be seen all over the United States. Mike speaks with a southern accent, not the standard American accent of many other reporters. Mike is worried that he will not get the job because of his accent. What should Mike do?

Situation 2

Julia is a high school student. She grew up in Mexico and just moved to Spain. She feels self-conscious at school because her accent is different. She wants to fit in but she feels silly speaking with a Spanish accent because it doesn't feel natural. What should Julia do?

Situation 3

Angelique works as a salesperson in a French clothing store in Australia. She speaks fluent English with a French accent. Her boss likes the way she speaks. He thinks her accent helps sell clothing. Her friends like the way she speaks. They say her accent makes her different and special. Angelique has recently become an Australian citizen. She thinks she should change her accent to sound more Australian. What should Angelique do?

Situation 4

Sharon works for a financial company in a small city in Ireland. She recently hired Meir from India, who speaks an Indian dialect of English. Sharon is happy with Meir's work. However, there are problems between Meir and some people on her staff. These people are frustrated because they have a difficult time understanding Meir because of his accent. What should Sharon do?

Step 2: Beginning with the student who chose Situation 1, take turns leading a group discussion about the situation you chose. **The leader should make sure that every person participates.**

In each discussion:
- Talk about possible solutions for the situation (what the person *could* do).
- Decide which solution is best (what the person *should* do).

Step 3: Tell the class about the solution your group chose for each situation.

ALTERNATIVE SPEAKING TOPICS

Discuss one of the topics. Use the vocabulary and grammar from the unit.

1. Many governments have laws about which languages people can use. For example, some countries have one or more "official languages" that must be taught in school and spoken at work and in the government. Some countries do not allow certain languages to be spoken at all. What is the language policy in your country? Which languages or dialects are accepted? Which are not accepted? Why?

2. English has been described as a "world language." Many people all over the world speak English at school, in business, in politics, and in other situations. What are the advantages of having a world language? What are the disadvantages? What other languages do you think might become world languages in the future? Why?

RESEARCH TOPICS, see page 193.

UNIT
5

Culture and Commerce

Long-necked women from the Pa Daung tribe in Thailand, wearing brass coils around their necks

FOCUS ON THE TOPIC

A PREDICT

Discuss the questions with the class.

1. Look at the photo. Why do you think these women are wearing coils around their necks?

2. Read the title of the unit. *Commerce* means business. In your opinion, what is the relationship between culture and commerce in tourism?

73

B ⬤ SHARE INFORMATION

*Work in a small group. First, read each statement and decide your opinion. Write **SD** (strongly disagree), **D** (disagree), **A** (agree), or **SA** (strongly agree) in each blank. Then discuss your opinions with the group.*

_____ 1. Tourism can be harmful to people living in a tourist community.

_____ 2. Tourism can help people have a better life.

_____ 3. Tourist activities that harm people or the environment should not be allowed.

_____ 4. Any tourist activity that makes money should be allowed.

_____ 5. Tourism is a good way for people to make money.

_____ 6. Tourism destroys the natural environment.

C ⬤ BACKGROUND AND VOCABULARY

1 🎧 CD 2 44 *A travel blog (web log) is an Internet site where people write about their trips. Read and listen to the travel blog about a trip to Thailand.*

Travel Blog: Northern Thailand

We've had a great time exploring Northern Thailand so far. It's really interesting and there's so much to see!

One thing I've learned is that elephants are the national symbol of Thailand. They are very important in Thai history and cultural **(1) traditions**. Elephants are also a big tourist **(2) attraction**, so there are many different elephant parks for tourists to visit. We decided to visit one, but we soon found out that there is a lot of
(3) controversy about them. Some parks treat the elephants very badly. They are not treated with respect and have to perform **(4) degrading** tricks for tourists, like playing basketball and dancing. The owners don't really care about the elephants; they just want to **(5) make a living** by showing the animals to tourists.

However, the elephant park we went to is very different. In this place, they are trying to **(6) preserve** the wild elephant

---

population. It's a large, beautiful park where the elephants can walk around freely. They are so playful! I took this photo of two young elephants walking together with their trunks **(7) wrapped** around each other, just like two kids walking hand-in-hand. Going to the park was an amazing experience, much better than seeing elephants in a **(8) zoo**. I also bought some nice **(9) souvenirs**: a stuffed elephant toy for my niece and a carved wooden elephant for my parents.

Tomorrow we're going to see another unusual sight: the village of Nai Soi where the long-necked women of the Pa Daung tribe live. The women wear brass coils to **(10) stretch** their necks. More on that tomorrow!

2 *Write the number of each boldfaced word or phrase in the text next to its definition.*

_____ **a.** disagreement among people

_____ **b.** a place where animals are kept so that people can look at them

_____ **c.** to keep something from being changed or harmed

_____ **d.** customs (special activities) that have existed for a long time

_____ **e.** things you buy to help you remember a place

_____ **f.** to make something longer by pulling it

_____ **g.** folded around something

_____ **h.** showing no respect

_____ **i.** something interesting to see or do

_____ **j.** to earn money from

A **LISTENING ONE: Tourist Attraction or Human Zoo?**

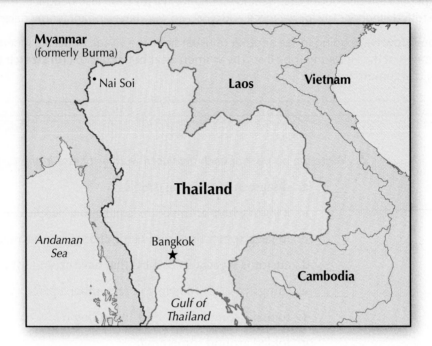

🎧 CD 7 *You will hear a news report about the village of the long-necked women in Thailand.*
45 *Listen to this excerpt from the report. Circle your prediction.*

This news report will present the tourist attraction in _____.

    a. a positive way
    b. a negative way
    c. a way that is both positive and negative

◖LISTEN FOR MAIN IDEAS

🎧 CD 7
46 *Listen to the radio news report. Write **T** (true) or **F** (false) for each statement.*

The tradition of the long-necked women . . .

_____ **1.** started in Thailand.

_____ **2.** brings tourists to the village to buy souvenirs and take pictures.

_____ **3.** allows women to earn money for their families.

_____ **4.** is safe and healthy for the women.

_____ **5.** has caused controversy among tourists.

_____ **6.** will continue as long as tourists keep coming.

◖ LISTEN FOR DETAILS

CD 1
47 *Listen again. Circle the best answer to complete each statement.*

1. About _____ tourists visit the long-necked women every year.
   a. 1,000
   b. 10,000
   c. 100,000

2. When they lived in Myanmar, the Pa Daung _____.
   a. sold souvenirs to tourists
   b. fought in a war
   c. were farmers

3. A full set of brass coils _____.
   a. weighs up to 22 pounds
   b. costs up to $22
   c. takes up to 22 years to put on

4. A long-necked woman cannot remove the coils because _____.
   a. her neck is very weak
   b. she won't make any money
   c. her family won't let her

5. Back in Myanmar, the tradition of stretching women's necks _____.
   a. has almost disappeared
   b. is still strong
   c. is becoming more popular

6. A long-necked woman can make $70 to $80 _____ from tourists.
   a. a week
   b. a month
   c. a year

7. Sandra feels that she is helping the Pa Daung women because she is _____.
   a. spending money in the village
   b. not visiting the village
   c. bringing food to the village

8. Fredrick uses the image of _____ to describe the Pa Daung women.
   a. animals in a zoo
   b. prisoners in jail
   c. actors in a show

◀ MAKE INFERENCES

Listen to excerpts from the report. Choose adjectives from the list to describe the speaker's tone of voice and take notes on word choices. Then decide whether the person would agree or disagree with the statement.

accepting	argumentative	confused	frustrated	lucky
angry	confident	contented	homesick	sad

⟨CD 7⟩ ㊽ Excerpt One: Pa Peiy

Tone of voice: *sad, accepting*

Word choice: *OK = not great*

Pa Peiy would (agree / (disagree)) with the statement:

"I like wearing the neck coils."

⟨CD 7⟩ ㊾ Excerpt Two: Ma Nang

Tone of voice: _____

Word choice: _____

Ma Nang would (agree / disagree) with the statement:

"I'm happy that the tourists come to look at me."

⟨CD 7⟩ ㊿ Excerpt Three: Sandra

Tone of voice: _____

Word choice: _____

Sandra would (agree / disagree) with the statement:

"I'm worried about how tourism affects the Pa Daung."

⟨CD 7⟩ ㉛ Excerpt Four: Fredrick

Tone of voice: _____

Word choice: _____

Fredrick would (agree / disagree) with the statement:

"I don't like the tradition of neck stretching."

◀ EXPRESS OPINIONS

Discuss the statements in a small group. Do you agree or disagree? Explain your opinions.

1. I would like to visit the women of the Pa Daung tribe.

2. The Pa Daung women are helped by the tourism in their village.

1 Look at the information about Cape Cod. What can you conclude about this tourist destination?

Cape Cod, Massachusetts

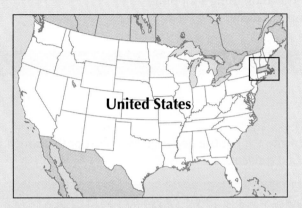 

Cape Cod is one of New England's most popular tourist attractions, with more than 5 million tourists visiting each year. During the summer season, from June to September, tourists come to relax at the beach, shop in the small towns, and eat fresh seafood. During the rest of the year, the population drops to about 200,000. Many summer businesses, such as restaurants and souvenir shops, close for the winter.

2 CD 1 Listening Two is an excerpt from a town hall meeting. The mayor (the town leader)
52 is leading the meeting. The townspeople are listening and expressing their opinions. Listen and circle the best answer to complete each sentence. Compare your answers with a partner's.

1. The traffic on Cape Cod _____.
   a. gets worse during the summer
   b. is bad all year
   c. is better now that there are buses

2. _____ is difficult to find on Cape Cod.
   a. Low-priced housing
   b. Housing for families
   c. Vacation housing

3. The restaurant owner knows a waitress who lives _____.
   a. in her car
   b. far from her work
   c. in a hotel

(continued on next page)

4. The woman who runs the souvenir shop says _____.

    a. she plans to open another store next year in a neighboring village

    b. she does most of her business during the summer

    c. her business is doing badly this year

5. The business owner says he lost money because _____.

    a. too many stores are selling the same things

    b. tourists go to the beach instead of going shopping

    c. the rainy weather kept tourists away

C INTEGRATE LISTENINGS ONE AND TWO

STEP 1: Organize

1 *Work with a partner. In the chart, write the positive and negative effects of tourism on the Pa Daung tribe and the Cape Cod residents.*

EFFECTS OF TOURISM		
	Positive Effects	**Negative Effects**
Pa Daung Tribe		Women continue to wrap their necks.
Cape Cod Residents	Tourists spend money.	

2 *Draw a circle around the effects that are similar in both communities.*

STEP 2: Synthesize

With your partner, debate the topic "Does tourism help or hurt people in tourist communities?"

Student A: take the pro position (Tourism has positive effects on people in tourist communities).

Student B: take the con position (Tourism has negative effects on people in tourist communities).

Each person has two to three minutes to present his or her position. Use the information from Step 1 to support your position. Then switch partners.

Useful Language

- I think tourism helps / hurts tourist communities because . . .
- For example, in Thailand / Cape Cod . . .
- One tourist / Pa Daung woman / Cape Cod resident said . . .
- Also . . .
- Another argument for / against tourism is . . .

3 FOCUS ON SPEAKING

A VOCABULARY

REVIEW

Cross out the word that doesn't belong in each group. Consult a dictionary if necessary.

Example

zoo	~~museum~~	animal park	wildlife center
1. afford	have money for	pay for	borrow from
2. controversy	argument	debate	agreement
3. depend on	rely on	need	choose
4. degrading	polite	embarrassing	painful
5. make a living	earn money	enjoy life	get paid
6. preserve	destroy	save	care for
7. season	days of the week	time of year	period of time
8. souvenir	reminder	keepsake	equipment
9. stretch	enlarge	make longer	reduce
10. tourist attraction	place to see	guidebook	point of interest
11. tradition	habit	change	belief
12. village	small town	community	city
13. wrap	open	cover	surround

EXPAND

1 *Read the letter to the editor about the effects of tourism in Cape Cod.*

TO THE EDITOR:

Effects of Tourism

Millions of tourists visit Cape Cod each year. Most tourists come here to relax at the beach and enjoy our delicious seafood. Others like to **get off the beaten path** and explore parts of the Cape that most tourists don't see. Whatever they do here, we appreciate the tourists because most **locals** have jobs that depend on tourism, such as shop owners and restaurant workers.

(continued on next page)

However, tourism can also have a negative **impact** on the area. The cost of housing is one example. The cost of housing keeps increasing, so many families can't afford to buy a home. **In the long run**, this problem will force families to leave the Cape and live elsewhere.

Problems like this affect our **way of life** here on the Cape. Life is becoming more difficult for the year-round residents. We need to **find a compromise** that will preserve the tourist income for the area and allow the locals to continue living here.

Michelle Connelly
Sandwich, Mass.

2 *Match the words and phrases on the left with the definitions on the right.*

_____ **1.** get off the beaten path

_____ **2.** locals

_____ **3.** impact

_____ **4.** in the long run

_____ **5.** way of life

_____ **6.** find a compromise

a. the effect of a situation

b. customs and habits of daily living

c. far in the future

d. go somewhere that most tourists don't visit

e. look for ideas that two groups of people can share

f. people who live in a particular place

◖ **CREATE**

Work in a small group. Each person thinks of a tourist destination he or she has visited. Take turns making a short presentation about the destination. Answer the questions in your presentation. Use the vocabulary from the box.

1. What tourist destination did you visit?

2. What are the major tourist attractions?

3. What impact does tourism have on the locals?

4. What impact does tourism have on the environment?

afford	find a compromise	preserve
controversial	get off the beaten path	season
degrading	in the long run	souvenir
depend on	locals	way of life
	make a living	

1 Work with a partner. Read the conversation between two residents of Cape Cod. Then switch roles and repeat.

A: Did you see the weather report today? They say it**'ll** keep raining all week.

B: Really? That's bad. **If it keeps raining**, the tourists **won't** come. They**'ll** stay home.

A: I know. I**'ll probably** lose money this week.

FUTURE PREDICTIONS WITH *IF*-CLAUSES	
1. Use *will* + base form and *will not* (*won't*) + base form to make predictions about the future. *Will* is usually contracted in speech.	It **will rain** again next week. Tourists **won't come** to the shops and restaurants. They**'ll stay** home.
2. Use *probably* with *will*. *Probably* comes between *will* and the main verb. In a negative sentence, *probably* comes before *won't*.	Business **will probably be** slow all week. I **probably won't make** enough money.
3. Use *if-clauses* to talk about possible results in the future. In the main clause, use *will* + base form. In the *if-clause*, use simple present. The *if-clause* can come before or after the main clause. When it comes first, use a comma between the clauses.	If the rain **continues**, we**'ll have** a lot of problems. ⎵_if-clause_⎵ ⎵_main clause_⎵ We**'ll have** a lot of problems if the rain **continues**. ⎵_main clause_⎵ ⎵_if-clause_⎵

2 Complete the sentences using the words in parentheses. Use contractions of **will** where possible.

1. If it _____rains_____ a lot this summer, fewer tourists _____will visit_____.
   (rain)   (visit)

   Businesses ___probably won't make___ enough money. Some shops
              (probably / not / make)

   ___will probably close___.
   (probably / close)

2. If housing _____ (get) more expensive, many families

_____ (not / be able to) afford a house on Cape Cod. Some families

_____ (probably / move away), and others _____ (continue) renting.

3. I heard that another seafood restaurant _____ (probably / open) in town. If it

_____ (open), there _____ (be) more jobs for the locals. But

the other restaurants in town _____ (probably / lose) customers.

4. Traffic _____ (get) worse if more tourists _____ (bring) their

cars to Cape Cod. There _____ (probably / not / be) enough parking spaces at the

beach.

3 *Work with a partner. Read about the people who live and vacation on Cape Cod.*

CAPE COD PORTRAITS

Joe . . .
- owns Joe's Seafood Shack.
- serves 100 pounds of seafood each day.
- employs five cooks and four waitresses.

Bill & Maureen . . .
- own the Cape Art Gallery.
- sell paintings and jewelry from local artists.
- employ two sales clerks.

Sandy . . .
- is a high school student.
- works in a local souvenir shop during the summer.
- saves money to go to college.

The Harvey family . . .
- vacations on Cape Cod every summer.
- rents a house from a local.
- enjoys the area because the beaches aren't crowded.

Take turns making predictions about the future. What will happen to these people if tourism increases on Cape Cod? What will happen if tourism decreases?

Example

STUDENT A: What **will happen** to Joe if tourism increases?
STUDENT B: If tourism **increases**, Joe's restaurant **will probably get** busier.
STUDENT A: You're right. He**'ll serve** more seafood every day. He**'ll probably need** to hire more cooks and waitresses. . . .

◀ **PRONUNCIATION: Words Spelled with o**

The letter *o* has many different pronunciations in English. In the five words *hotel, shop, come, woman,* and *move,* the letter *o* has five different pronunciations. Sometimes the letters around *o* can help you guess how to pronounce the vowel, but not always.

CD 1
53 Listen to how *o* is pronounced in the underlined words.

The long-necked women of Pa Daung talk with tourists, pose for pictures, and sell souvenirs. They have become an important source of commerce and money in small villages along the Thai/Myanmar border.

Is the letter *o* pronounced the same in any of the underlined words?

SOME SPELLING RULES FOR PRONOUNCING O	
Spelling	**Pronunciation**
o followed by a consonant and silent e *home, bone, pose, hope, close*	/ow/, like the vowel in *go*. Keep rounding your lips.
o followed by consonants *shop, lot, job, commerce, problem*	/a/, like the vowel in *father*; this vowel has no "o" sound. Do not round your lips.
o followed by *ng, ss, st, ll, ff* *long, boss, lost, collar, office*	/ɔ/, like the vowel in *law*. This vowel is like /a/, but the lips are a little rounded. Some Americans pronounce these words with /a/, like the vowel in *father*. You can use this vowel, too.
Exceptions	**Pronunciation**
come, mother, brother, love, other	/ə/, like the vowel in *cut*. Your mouth is almost closed.
move, lose	/uw/, like the vowel in *do*
woman	/ʊ/, like the vowel in *could*
women	/ɪ/, like the vowel in *sit*

1 Listen to the words and repeat them.

1. positive	7. most	13. controversy
2. progress	8. money	14. sold
3. economic	9. vote	15. option
4. modern	10. popular	16. hospital
5. proposal	11. company	17. ocean
6. month	12. local	18. done

2 Work with a partner. How is the letter **o** pronounced in the words in Exercise 1? Write each word under one of the columns. The number in parentheses tells you how many words are in that column. Ask your teacher to repeat the words if you're not sure. Check your words with the class.

O SOUNDS LIKE . . .		
the vowel in *father* (8)	**the vowel in *go* (6)**	**the vowel in *cut* (4)**
positive		

3 Make phrases by writing words from the box in the blanks. Check your answers with a partner's. Practice saying the phrases to your partner. Pronounce the vowels carefully.

~~economic~~	local	modern	popular	positive

1. _____economic_____ progress (business, jobs)

2. _____ controversy (not in earlier times)

3. _____ proposal (one that will have good results)

4. _____ **o**ption (one people like)

5. _____ **co**mpany (in this area)

◀ FUNCTION: Making Suggestions

When you make a suggestion, you say what you think someone should do. Suggestions can be *stronger*, when you strongly believe the other person should follow your advice, or *weaker*, when you don't feel as strongly.

1 *Read the conversation between two tourists in Thailand. Which suggestions are stronger? Which are weaker?*

A: What do you want to do tomorrow? **One option is to** visit an elephant park.

B: That's a great idea! Then **we could** go to Pa Duang to see the long-necked women.

A: **Let's not** go there. I think it's degrading for the women.

B: OK, but **we definitely shouldn't** miss the elephant park.

MAKING SUGGESTIONS		
Stronger	We should (definitely) . . . We (definitely) shouldn't . . . Let's (not) . . . I think / don't think we should . . .	visit an elephant park.
Weaker	One option is to . . . We might (not) want to . . . We could . . . Why don't we . . .	visit an elephant park.
	What do you think of . . . How about . . .	visiting an elephant park?

2 *Read the suggestions. Circle the one that is stronger. Discuss the difference between the two suggestions.*

1. a. Let's take a guided tour.

 b. How about taking a guided tour?

2. a. We might want to buy souvenirs.

 b. We should definitely buy souvenirs.

3. a. I think we should eat at the hotel.

 b. One option is to eat at the hotel.

(continued on next page)

4. a. We could go to the elephant park today.

    b. Let's not go to the elephant park today.

5. a. What do you think of visiting the long-necked women?

    b. I don't think we should visit the long-necked women.

3 *Work with a partner. Imagine that you are going to spend four days in Bangkok, Thailand. What would you like to do? Read the list of activity choices and take turns making suggestions.*

ACTIVITY CHOICES

Animals

- Go to Dusit Zoo to see wild animals.
- Visit the Snake Farm and see venom¹ removed from snakes to make medicine.
- Volunteer at an elephant park and help take care of the elephants.

Sightseeing

- Go to the National Museum and learn about Thai art.
- Visit the Grand Palace to see where Thai kings lived.
- Go to the Wat Sai floating market, where farmers sell food on boats.

Shopping

- Buy books about Thailand from Asia Books.
- Find fashionable women's clothing at Siam Square shops.
- Go to Lao Song Handicrafts to buy traditional Thai crafts and souvenirs.

Off the Beaten Path

- Spend a day at a spa, enjoying a massage, skin care, and a sauna.
- Take a Thai cooking class at the Blue Elephant Cooking School.
- Go on a bike tour of Bangkok.

¹**venom:** poisonous liquid that snakes produce

◖ PRODUCTION: Simulation

In this activity, you will *participate in a simulation—an activity that reflects a real-life situation*. In this simulation about the effects of tourism, you will talk about a controversial proposal to build a hotel in a rainforest. You will need to negotiate your ideas and reach a compromise. Try to use the vocabulary, grammar, pronunciation, and language for making suggestions that you learned in the unit.*

Read the situation on page 89 about a company that wants to build a hotel. Then complete the activity.

*For Alternative Speaking Topics, see page 91.

Royal Hotels wants to build a large 300-room resort hotel on Coral Beach, a quiet beach next to a small fishing village. Coral Beach only has a few tourists now, but the company has studied the area and thinks it can be a popular tourist attraction. Tourists can:

- enjoy the beautiful beaches
- visit the local fishing village
- explore the nearby rainforest

The proposal is controversial. In order to build the resort, Royal Hotels would need to build a road through the rainforest. The rainforest is a protected area that is managed by Landwatch, an environmental group. Landwatch is worried about the impact the hotel will have on the environment and wildlife. In addition, local residents in the fishing village are worried about the negative impact on their way of life.

Step 1: Work in three groups. Group A takes the point of view of representatives of Royal Hotels, Group B takes the point of view of the Landwatch group, and Group C takes the point of view of the local villagers. Read your group's position below and on page 90. **Do not read other groups' positions.** Talk about the positive and negative impacts of the hotel. Take notes.

Group A: Royal Hotels

Your group represents the needs and wants of tourists visiting the area.
- In order to build the hotel, Royal Hotels needs permission from Landwatch to build a road through the rainforest.
- The hotel needs workers in the hotel (restaurants, shops, etc.) and to run tourist services such as area and fishing tours.
- In a hotel survey, tourists said they want to:
  - visit natural areas like the ocean and the jungle, and see wildlife
  - go to nice, clean beaches
  - eat at good restaurants
  - see life in a traditional fishing village
  - go sport fishing
- Royal Hotels is willing to spend one million dollars to preserve natural areas and/or help the fishing village.

Group B: Landwatch

Your group represents the needs of the environment: the protection of the animals, sea life, plants, land, water, and air.

- Because the population is small, the area has very little pollution.
- Some villagers make money by hunting wild animals in the rainforest and selling them to restaurants in other cities. Landwatch wants to preserve the wildlife. It wants locals to stop hunting the animals, but the locals need the extra money.
- The fishermen have taken too many fish from the ocean. Landwatch wants them to catch fewer fish and let the fish population grow again.
- Landwatch needs money to continue its rainforest research and to teach the locals how to preserve the environment.

Group C: Locals

Your group represents the needs of local residents.

- People in the village live a traditional way of life. The culture is based on their lives as fishermen, with many rituals, crafts, and customs. Some people are afraid these traditions will be lost if the village changes.
- The fishermen use the Coral Beach to bring in their fishing boats.
- There is a high unemployment rate in the village. There are fewer fish in the ocean now, so there is less work for the fishermen. There are not many other jobs for people in the village.
- The village is not well developed. It needs better roads and utilities (water, electricity, phones). The nearest hospital is a three-hour drive, and most villagers don't have cars. There is a small school, but it needs more teachers and supplies (textbooks, paper, pencils, etc.).
- Some villagers earn extra money by hunting wild animals in the rainforest and selling them to restaurants in the city. Landwatch is trying to stop people from doing this, but the locals need the extra money.

Step 2: Form new groups of three, one student from Group A, one from Group B, and one from Group C. Each student explains the point of view of the group he or she is representing, (for example, "I represent Royal Hotels and we think . . ."). Work together to find a compromise proposal. Take notes in the chart.

COMPROMISE PROPOSAL		
The hotel will . . .	**Landwatch will . . .**	**The villagers will . . .**

Step 3: Present the compromise proposals to the whole class.

ALTERNATIVE SPEAKING TOPICS

Discuss one of the topics. Use the vocabulary and grammar from the unit.

1. If you were a travel agent in Thailand, would you book tours to see the long-necked women? Why or why not?

2. For some countries, tourism is the most important way for the country to make money. For example, Thailand used to make most of its money from growing rice, but now more money comes from tourism. What are the pros and cons of this?

RESEARCH TOPICS, see page 194.

UNIT
6

The Art of Storytelling

① FOCUS ON THE TOPIC

Ⓐ PREDICT

Discuss the questions with the class.

1. What's happening in the photo?

2. Read the title of the unit. Why is storytelling an art? How is it similar to the art of painting or dancing?

93

People have told stories for thousands of years as a form of entertainment. Today we can also read stories in books or watch them in movies or on TV.

Discuss the questions with a partner.

1. Did anyone tell you stories when you were a child? Who told the stories? What kind of stories did you hear?

2. What do you like about different kinds of storytelling? Which types do you like best? Why?
   - listening to someone tell a story
   - reading a book
   - seeing a movie
   - watching a play

C BACKGROUND AND VOCABULARY

1 Read and listen to the preview of a story by Jackie Torrence.

One of America's best known storytellers was Jackie Torrence. Her stories came from old American and African-American folktales.

Every year, Robert's town had a spring **(1) social** in the town hall. There was a band with music and dancing. Robert was going to drive to the dance with his friend David. This year, Robert didn't have a **(2) date** for the dance. He had asked several girls to go with him, but none of them could go.

On the day of the social, Robert got ready for the dance. The day **(3) wore on** slowly, and it seemed like the evening would never come.

Finally, it was time to go. Robert drove to his friend's house to pick him up. He turned the corner and the lights from his car **(4) fell on** the house. As he **(5) approached** the house, he saw David waving to him from the kitchen window. Robert felt **(6) chilled** when he got out of the car, for the air was cold. Before they left, David's parents told him to come home at 12 midnight. His parents were **(7) strict**, so he knew that he couldn't be late.

At last, Robert and David started down the highway on the way to the social. . . .

2 *Match each boldfaced word or phrase in the text with its definition or synonym.*

_____ **a.** passed very slowly

_____ **b.** came closer to

_____ **c.** cold

_____ **d.** shone on

_____ **e.** partner

_____ **f.** party

_____ **g.** expecting others to obey rules

3 *Look at the picture. Write the letter next to the corresponding word. Consult a dictionary if necessary.*

_____ **1.** cemetery

_____ **2.** driveway

_____ **3.** gravestone

_____ **4.** headlights

_____ **5.** picket fence

_____ **6.** weeds

②FOCUS ON LISTENING

Ⓐ LISTENING ONE: Lavender

CD 2
③ *You will hear the story "Lavender[1]," told by storyteller Jackie Torrence. Listen to the beginning of the story. What do you think will happen to Robert and David? Discuss your predictions with a partner.*

1. They will meet someone.

2. They will see something strange.

3. They will get lost.

◖ LISTEN FOR MAIN IDEAS

CD 2
④ *Listen to the story. Write answers to the questions. You do not need to write full sentences. Discuss your answers with the class.*

1. Robert and David go to a spring social. Who do they meet while driving down the highway? _____

2. What does Robert give to Lavender at the dance? _____

3. Where do Robert and David take Lavender after the dance? _____

4. Where do Robert and David go the next day? _____

5. What do Robert and David discover about Lavender at the end of the story?

   _____

◖ LISTEN FOR DETAILS

CD 2
⑤ *Listen again. Put the events from the story in order. Write 1 next to the first event, 2 next to the second event, and so on.*

_____ **a.** Robert and David saw a girl wearing a lavender evening dress.

_____ **b.** They noticed that the windows on the house were broken.

_____ **c.** Robert and David realized that they didn't have dates for the evening.

_____ **d.** Weeds and grass had grown up in Lavender's driveway.

_____ **e.** The name on the gravestone was *Lavender*.

_____ **f.** Lavender said that her parents were a little strict.

_____ **g.** Robert and David danced with Lavender.

Compare your answers with a partner's. Discuss any differences with the class.

_____

[1]The word *lavender* has several meanings: It is a kind of flower, a light purple color, and a female name.

◖ MAKE INFERENCES

Listen to the excerpts. Circle the two adjectives that best describe the character's emotions in each excerpt from the story. Write down key phrases or sentences that helped you to choose your answer.

	ADJECTIVES THAT DESCRIBE EMOTIONS	KEY PHRASES AND SENTENCES
Excerpt One CD 2 6	Robert feels . . . **a.** in love **b.** shy **c.** sad	
Excerpt Two CD 2 7	Robert feels . . . **a.** angry **b.** confused **c.** worried	
Excerpt Three CD 2 8	Robert and David feel . . . **a.** afraid **b.** lonely **c.** uncomfortable	

Discuss your answers in a small group. Explain why you chose certain adjectives.

◖ EXPRESS OPINIONS

Work in a small group. Discuss the questions.

1. When did you first think that something strange was happening in the story?

2. Were you surprised by the ending? Why or why not?

3. What makes Jackie Torrence a good storyteller? Was the story interesting? Why or why not?

B LISTENING TWO: How to Tell a Story

🔊 CD2
9 *You will hear another storyteller explain some techniques to use in storytelling. Match the techniques in column 1 with purposes for the techniques in column 2. Write the correct letter in the blank.*

Storytelling Technique

___c___ **1.** Change your voice

_____ **2.** Talk faster and louder

_____ **3.** Talk slowly and softly

_____ **4.** Use dialogue (people speaking)

_____ **5.** Use different voices for different characters

Purpose for Technique

a. to show the audience who is talking.

b. to sound scary.

~~c~~. to change the feeling of the story.

d. to make the story more exciting.

e. to bring the characters to life.

C INTEGRATE LISTENINGS ONE AND TWO

◀ **STEP 1: Organize**

🔊 CD2
10 *Listen to the excerpts from Make Inferences again. Identify the techniques (from Listening Two) that Jackie Torrence uses. Write the letters in the blanks. There may be more than one technique in each excerpt.*

EXCERPTS FROM LISTENING ONE	TECHNIQUES FROM LISTENING TWO
Excerpt One Techniques used: _____ **Excerpt Two** Techniques used: _____ **Excerpt Three** Techniques used: _____	**a.** Talk faster and louder. **b.** Talk slowly and softly. **c.** Use dialogue. **d.** Use different voices.

◖ STEP 2: Synthesize

Work with a partner. Discuss the excerpts from Step 1. Talk about (1) the technique(s) in the excerpt and (2) the purpose of the technique(s). Agree or disagree and explain your opinions. Switch partners and repeat.

Useful Language

- In this excerpt Jackie Torrence . . .
- This excerpt is an example of . . .
- Jackie Torrence uses this technique to . . .
- The reason Jackie Torrence uses this technique is because . . .

To Agree with a Statement:

- I agree . . .
- I think you're right . . .

To Disagree with a Statement:

- I disagree. I think . . .
- I don't think so. I think . . .

③ FOCUS ON SPEAKING

Ⓐ VOCABULARY

◖ REVIEW

Choose the correct answer to the question with the boldfaced word or phrase.

1. What happens when you **approach** a building?
   a. you get closer to it
   b. you leave it
   c. you walk around inside it

2. What do **strict** parents want their children to do?
   a. to be funny
   b. to follow the rules
   c. to tell stories

3. Where would a couple go on a **date**?
   a. to a hospital
   b. to the movies
   c. to work

(continued on next page)

4. What is a **driveway**?

   a. a road leading up to a house
   b. a sign that tells people where to drive
   c. a place where people cannot walk

5. What would probably happen at a spring social as the evening **wears on**?

   a. people get the food ready and put up decorations
   b. people start arriving at the social
   c. people begin to go home

6. What would a storyteller probably see in an **audience**?

   a. people
   b. animals
   c. furniture

7. Which of the following stories is probably **scary**?

   a. a funny story
   b. a ghost story
   c. a love story

8. Which of the following is an example of **dialogue**?

   a. "I'm going to eat you," said the bear. "Leave me alone!" said the boy.
   b. The bear chased the boy, and the boy ran away.
   c. The bear said he would eat the boy. The boy told the bear to go away.

9. What are the **characters** in a story?

   a. the events in the story
   b. the location where the story takes place
   c. the people (or animals) in the story

10. What happens when a dog **chases** a cat?

    a. the dog runs after the cat
    b. the dog sits down next to the cat
    c. the cat runs after the dog

◖ EXPAND

Read an excerpt from a story about a little boy and a bear. Notice the verbs that show how each character is speaking. Match each verb with its meaning.

"Stop!" (**1**) **yelled** the bear. The sound scared the boy so much that he stopped running.

"What are you going to do to me?" he (**2**) **whispered**, his voice so soft that the bear almost couldn't hear it.

"That's a very good question," (**3**) **growled** the bear.

_____ **a.** to speak very quietly

_____ **b.** to speak in a low, angry voice

_____ **c.** to speak loudly

"Are you going to eat me?" (**4**) **asked** the little boy.

The bear just looked at him, showing his big white teeth. The boy (**5**) **repeated** his question.

"So, are you going to eat me?" The bear didn't answer, so the boy (**6**) **continued**, "Because if you are, I'd like to write a note to my parents to say goodbye."

"You look very tasty," the bear (**7**) **replied**, "but no, I'm not going to eat you."

_____ **d.** to request that someone tell you something

_____ **e.** to say something after a pause or interruption

_____ **f.** to answer a question

_____ **g.** to say something again

◖ CREATE

Work with a partner. Choose three words from the lists. Each word should come from a different box. Create a short conversation that uses all three words.

ask / reply	afraid	approach	audience
continue	happy	as the morning / day / night wore on	character
growl	sad	chase	dialogue
say / repeat	scary	go on a date	driveway
whisper	strict		weeds
yell	worried		

Example

STUDENT A: Is this your house?
STUDENT B: Shhh. You need to <u>whisper</u>. My parents are really <u>strict</u>.
STUDENT A: So you don't want them to know that we <u>went on a date</u>?
STUDENT B: Right!

Perform your conversation for the class. The audience listens and identifies the three words you chose. Then repeat the activity with three different words.

1 *Read the paragraph and underline the infinitive verbs (**to + base form**). Then answer the questions. Discuss your answers with a partner.*

Storytellers change their voices <u>to change</u> the feeling of a story. For example, they may speak faster in order to make the story more exciting. They also use different character voices in order not to confuse the audience. Why do storytellers use these techniques? They use them to make their stories more interesting.

a. Why do storytellers change their voices?

b. Why do they speak faster sometimes?

c. Why do they use different character voices?

d. Why are these techniques important?

INFINITIVES OF PURPOSE	
I. Use an **infinitive of purpose** to explain the purpose of an action. • Use **to + base form**. • Use *in order to* **+ base form**. It often answers the question **Why**?	Storytellers change their voices **to change** the feeling of a story. They can speak faster **in order to make** the story more exciting. **A: Why** do storytellers use these techniques? **B:** They use them **to make** their stories more interesting.
2. Use *in order not to* **+ base form** to explain a negative purpose. In informal speech, you can also use **because + a reason** to express a negative purpose.	They also use different character voices **in order not to confuse** the audience. They also use different character voices **because** they don't want to confuse the audience.
3. *To* **+ base form** is more common in informal speech. *In order to* **+ base form** is more common in formal speech and writing.	The students will sit in the front row **to hear** the storyteller better. The students will sit in the front row **in order to hear** the storyteller better.

2 *Work with a partner. Match each action with its purpose.*

Action

_e_   **1.** Robert and David went to the social because they

_____   **2.** On the way, they stopped on the road because they

_____   **3.** They asked if Lavender was going to the social because they

_____   **4.** Lavender borrowed Robert's coat because she

_____   **5.** After the social, they dropped Lavender off at the top of the driveway because they

_____   **6.** Robert let Lavender keep his coat because he

_____   **7.** The next day, Robert and David went back to Lavender's house because they

Purpose

a. didn't want to make her parents angry.

b. wanted to get warm.

c. wanted an excuse to see her again.

d. wanted to find her.

e. wanted to have fun.

f. didn't want to go to the dance without a date.

g. wanted to give Lavender a ride.

For each match, combine the action and the reason into one sentence that contains an infinitive of purpose. Take turns saying the sentences. Listen to each other's sentences and correct any mistakes.

Example

STUDENT A: Robert and David went to the social to had some fun.
STUDENT B: I think it should be "to <u>have</u> some fun."
STUDENT A: Oh yeah! "Robert and David went to the social to have some fun."

3 *Work with the same partner. Discuss the reasons why a storyteller might use the following storytelling techniques. Begin your answer with "A storyteller might ..." and use infinitives of purpose.*

Question: Why would a storyteller . . .

  a. talk in a loud voice?

  b. talk quickly?

  c. talk very slowly and quietly?

  d. use different voices?

  e. move around while telling a story?

Answer: A storyteller might talk in a loud voice **to get** the audience's attention or **to sound** scary.

◀ PRONUNCIATION: Rhythm of Prepositional Phrases

A prepositional phrase consists of a preposition (P) and a noun phrase (NP).

Example

      P   NP

They drove to the social.

RHYTHM OF PREPOSITIONAL PHRASES	
Short prepositions: *to, at, in, of, on, with, for, from* are not stressed in prepositional phrases.	Lavender rode in their car. They danced with Lavender.
Unstressed prepositions join closely to the other words in a prepositional phrase. (In the example, the prepositional phrases and single words have the same stress pattern.)	for breakfast forbidden in the rain unafraid
Some prepositions have reduced pronunciations: The vowel is pronounced /ə/ in speaking.	**at home** /ət/ **for dinner** /fər/; rhymes with *her* **to school** *to* is usually /tə/; sounds like *t'school* **in town** /ən/ or /ɪn/

1 🔊 *Listen to the sentences. Complete the sentences with the prepositions you hear.*

1. Robert and David drove _____ their house.

2. Lavender was waiting _____ the road.

3. She walked _____ Robert.

4. The three friends went _____ the dance.

5. They got back _____ the car.

6. Robert and David were looking _____ the coat in the backyard.

7. Robert pointed _____ the gravestone.

8. They ran _____ the car.

Compare your answers with a partner's. Take turns saying the sentences aloud. Try to use the /ə/ sound when appropriate.

2 *Read the phrases aloud to yourself. Match each phrase in column 1 to a phrase in column 2 that has a similar stress pattern. Write the letters in the blanks.*

Column 1

_____ 1. come to dinner

_____ 2. Thanks for getting a job.

_____ 3. It's hard to dance.

_____ 4. a fortune at school

_____ 5. at nine

_____ 6. point at Tom

Column 2

a. a fortunate school

b. pointed top

c. It's cold today.

d. come tomorrow

e. Hank's forgetting his job.

f. arrive

🔊 *Listen to the answers. Did you match the columns correctly? Repeat the phrases after your teacher.*

Work with a partner. Student A reads a phrase from column 1. Student B reads the matching phrase in column 2. Switch columns and repeat.

◀ **FUNCTION: Transitions for Storytelling**

Transition words and phrases give information about the time when events happen in a story.

1 *Read the excerpt from the story of the boy and the bear. Notice the boldfaced transition words.*

(1) There was once a little boy who lived on the edge of a deep, dark forest[1]. **(2) One day** the little boy decided to go for a walk in the forest, where it was quiet and peaceful. **(3) After a while** he came to a part of the forest that he had never seen before. He turned around and realized that he didn't know where he was. "Oh no!" he whispered to himself. "I'm lost!" **(4) Suddenly**, he heard a noise behind him. He turned around and found himself face to face with a huge black bear!

Write the numbers of the transitions in the blanks.

Which transition(s) . . .

a. introduce the beginning of the story? (There are two.) _____ and _____

b. shows a quick change in the story? _____

c. shows that time passed? _____

---

[1]**forest:** area with many trees

TRANSITIONS FOR STORYTELLING

Use these transitions at the **beginning** of a story: To **begin a variety of stories** (real or magical): *This is a story about . . .* *One day / morning / evening . . .* To **begin magical or unreal stories**: *Once upon a time . . .* *There once was a _____ who . . .*	**This is a story about** the time I saw a bear in the forest. **Once upon a time** there was a boy who could fly.
Use these transitions in the **middle** of a story: *After a while, . . .* *(Very) soon . . .* *After that, . . .* *Suddenly, . . .* *The next day / week / month / year, . . .* *Later that morning / evening / day, . . .*	**After a while,** I realized that I was lost. **Suddenly,** I heard a noise in the bushes. **The next day,** the boy went back to the forest to find the bear.
Use these transitions to **end** a story: To **end a variety of stories** (real or magical): *From then on, . . .* *And that was . . .* To **end magical or unreal stories**: *The moral¹ of this story is . . .* *And _____ lived happily ever after.*	**From then on,** whenever I walked in the woods, I always brought a cell phone in case of an emergency. **The moral of this story is** "Don't talk to strangers."

2 Work with a partner. Read the sentences from different stories. Write **Beg** next to the transition sentences from the beginning of the story, **Mid** for the ones from the middle, and **End** for the ones from the end.

Story 1

_____ **a.** From then on, I was more careful whenever I went into the forest.

_____ **b.** The next day, I went back to the forest to look for the bear.

_____ **c.** One day I went out for a walk in the forest.

_____ **d.** Suddenly, I heard a loud growl coming from the bushes behind me.

_____ **e.** This is a story about the time I saw a bear.

---
¹**moral:** a message or lesson that a story teaches

Story 2

_____ **a.** Later that day, the boy saw the bear again.

_____ **b.** And that was the last time the boy ever saw the bear.

_____ **c.** There was once a boy who lived near the forest.

_____ **d.** The moral of this story is "Be kind to others and they will be kind to you."

_____ **e.** After that, the boy decided to go to the woods to look for berries.

3 *Work with a partner. Look at the pictures to retell the story of "Lavender." Take turns telling the story. Use the suggested vocabulary if you like. Use transition words.*

social / dates / headlights / give a ride

chilled / coat

home / driveway / strict / kiss

cemetery / gravestones / coat

◖ PRODUCTION: Telling a Story

In this activity, you will **prepare a story and tell it to the class**. The story could be from your culture or one that you make up yourself. Try to use the vocabulary, grammar, pronunciation, and transitions you learned in the unit.*

Follow the steps.

Step 1: Think of a short story that will be interesting and entertaining for your audience. It could be exciting, scary, funny, or sad. It could have unexpected events or a moral, or it could have unusual characters.

Write an outline of your story on a piece of paper. Use the sample outline as a guide.

> Title of the story: _____
>
> Place where the story takes place: _____
>
> **Main characters** (name and description):
>
> 1. _____
>
> 2. _____
>
> 3. _____
>
> Etc.
>
> **Outline of events** (List the main events using words and phrases):
>
> 1. _____
>
> 2. _____
>
> 3. _____
>
> Etc.

Step 2: Use your outline to practice your story. Use the storytelling techniques discussed in this unit.

- Use your voice (loud / soft, high / low) to create feelings.
- Use dialogue to bring your characters to life.

After you have practiced on your own, meet with a partner and tell your story. Switch partners and tell your story again.

Step 3: Perform your story for the class. Be dramatic and have fun.

---

*For Alternative Speaking Topics, see page 109.

ALTERNATIVE SPEAKING TOPICS

Discuss one of the topics. Use the vocabulary and grammar from the unit.

1. Today, most stories are told through books and movies rather than through oral storytelling. What will people lose if the tradition of oral storytelling ends? What are the advantages and disadvantages of modern storytelling through books and movies?

2. There are some stories that are very similar from one culture to another. For example, almost every country in the world has a version of "Cinderella," a story about a poor girl who marries a prince. What do you think is the reason for this?

RESEARCH TOPICS, see page 194.

UNIT 7 Voluntary Simplicity

①FOCUS ON THE TOPIC

A PREDICT

Voluntary simplicity *means choosing to live a simple life. Look at the pictures and discuss the questions with the class.*

1. What are the people in the pictures doing to live simply?

2. Why do you think people choose to live simply?

111

Work in a small group. Look at the two ways of doing things and discuss the questions.

Which in each pair . . .

a. costs less?

b. is easier to use?

c. is better for the environment?

d. do most people in your country use?

1. Home heating	wood stove	gas or electric furnace
2. Drying clothes	clothesline	clothes dryer
3. Light	candles	electric lights
4. Cutting wood	hand saw	chainsaw
5. Baby diapers	cloth diapers	disposable diapers

1 Read and listen to the online message board about simplifying your life.

Voluntary Simplicity
Welcome to the message board for people who want to simplify their lives.
Please share your questions, ideas, and experience.

Discussion Topic: Trying to Simplify

Newbie101   I'm trying to simplify our life, but my family doesn't understand. They think I'm **(1) insane**! Any suggestions?

RayOnline   To simplify your life, first look carefully at your **(2) consumption habits**. Do you buy things you don't really need? I don't go to shopping malls anymore because it's a **(3) slippery slope**. I buy one thing, and I want to buy more and more. It's hard to stop.

FarmerJohn   It's important to support businesses in the **(4) local economy**. Instead of shopping at big chain stores[1], shop at stores owned by people in your community.

Oblio OH   My family started **(5) homesteading** five years ago. We bought an old house with a lot of land. We put in a wood stove so we don't have to use **(6) fossil fuels**. We also planted a big garden. It's been a lot of work, but we love living this way!

EarthMama   You can become more **(7) self-sufficient** by doing things for yourself. For example, use the resources of the **(8) natural world** around you. Grow vegetables. Keep chickens. Some families even keep a beehive to **(9) produce** honey!

PalomaP   Don't buy everything new. Buy used goods at **(10) secondhand** stores. It's fun and less expensive.

EarthMama   Walk more and drive less. It may take longer, but it's **(11) worth doing** because you'll get more exercise and create less pollution.

Lula2008   TURN OFF THE TV!! Advertisers are constantly telling us to buy, buy, buy. Try to **(12) convince** your kids to turn the TV off, too.

Newbie101   Thanks a lot, everyone! This really helps!

---

[1] **chain store:** one of a group of shops owned by the same company

2 *Circle the best answer to complete each statement.*

1. "They think I'm **insane**!" means they think she's _____.
    a. correct
    b. crazy
    c. intelligent

2. "Look carefully at your **consumption habits**" means think about _____.
    a. how many things you buy
    b. how much you eat
    c. how often you drive your car

3. A **slippery slope** is when people do something _____ and can't control themselves.
    a. they don't want to do
    b. they understand well
    c. they think is interesting

4. "It's important to support businesses in the **local economy**" means it's important to shop at stores that _____.
    a. are the biggest stores in the area
    b. are owned by people in the neighborhood
    c. have the lowest prices

5. When you start **homesteading**, you _____.
    a. fix your house so you can live a simpler lifestyle
    b. buy a house in an expensive neighborhood
    c. change all the furniture

6. Heating a house with **fossil fuels** means _____.
    a. using solar (sun) power
    b. burning oil or natural gas
    c. using water and wind power

7. You can become more **self-sufficient** by _____.
    a. making or growing things instead of buying them
    b. making your own decisions
    c. not shopping at supermarkets

8. The resources in the **natural world** include _____.
    a. houses and buildings
    b. land, plants, and animals
    c. cars and trains

9. To **produce** honey means to _____.
    a. like honey
    b. make honey
    c. sell honey

10. A **secondhand** store sells _____.
   a. clocks and watches
   b. things that have been used by someone else
   c. tools to help around the house

11. An activity is **worth doing** if it is _____.
   a. boring
   b. difficult
   c. useful

12. To **convince** someone to do something, you should _____.
   a. find out if they want to do it
   b. give them a good reason to do it
   c. help them do it

②FOCUS ON LISTENING

A LISTENING ONE: Urban Homesteaders

1 *CD 2* *You will hear a radio report about a family of urban homesteaders that lives in a poor, inner-city¹ neighborhood. Listen to the beginning of the report. Put a check (✓) next to the things you think will be mentioned in the listening.*

_____ working in the garden

_____ sawing wood

_____ making honey with a beehive

_____ going to the movies

_____ baking bread

_____ washing clothes

_____ building a house

2 *What do you think is unusual about Daniel Staub and Kristin Brennan's lifestyle? List at least one idea.*

_____

¹**inner city:** the part of a city near the middle, where the buildings are in bad condition and people are poor

◖LISTEN FOR MAIN IDEAS

CD2
15 *Listen to the whole report. Circle the best answer to complete each statement.*

1. Kristin Brennan and Daniel Staub are trying to live a _____ lifestyle.
   a. quiet
   b. relaxing
   c. self-sufficient

2. Brennan and Staub live in an inner-city neighborhood because they _____.
   a. can't afford a house in a rural area
   b. want people to learn from their simple lifestyle
   c. like living in the city

3. Brennan and Staub _____ their neighbors.
   a. don't talk to
   b. have problems with
   c. are friends with

4. Brennan and Staub enjoy being together as a family while they _____.
   a. cook special meals
   b. do work around the house
   c. go on trips

5. Brennan thinks that using the dryer even once would be a "slippery slope" because _____.
   a. her children might get hurt
   b. the electricity might go out
   c. she might want to use the dryer again

◖LISTEN FOR DETAILS

CD2
16 *Listen again. Write **T** (true) or **F** (false) for each statement.*

Daniel Staub and Kristin Brennan . . .

_____ 1. have chickens, a goat, and a beehive.

_____ 2. grow most of their own food and buy secondhand clothes.

_____ 3. don't own a car or use electricity in their house.

_____ 4. have asked their neighbors to change their consumption habits.

_____ 5. hope that other people will try living more simply.

_____ 6. show neighborhood children how to work in the garden.

_____ 7. pay someone to cut wood for their wood stove.

_____ 8. sometimes use the clothes dryer.

◖ MAKE INFERENCES

Listen to the excerpts. Circle one or more phrases that could complete each statement.

CD 2
⑰ Excerpt One

Brennan and Staub would probably go shopping for clothes at _____.

a. a shopping mall
b. a yard sale[1]
c. a designer or name-brand store

CD 2
⑱ Excerpt Two

Brennan and Staub would probably enjoy _____ together as a family.

a. watching TV
b. going for a walk
c. cleaning the house

CD 2
⑲ Excerpt Three

Brennan and Staub would probably want to own _____.

a. a clothesline
b. solar lights (powered by the sun)
c. a refrigerator

Compare your answers with a classmate's. Explain your inferences using details from the report.

◖ EXPRESS OPINIONS

Discuss the questions in a small group.

1. Brennan and Staub both could live a more comfortable lifestyle but have chosen not to. Do you admire them for their voluntary simplicity (choice to live simply), or do you think it's strange? Explain your opinion.

2. How is your lifestyle similar to or different from Brennan and Staub's lifestyle? Do you live this way by choice or by necessity (because you have to)?

---

[1]**yard sale:** a sale of used items from someone's house that takes place in front of his or her house

1 *Read the information about the Shakers, an eighteenth-century religious group who chose to live simply.*

The Shakers were a religious group that formed in Britain in the 1700s. They came to the United States so they could be free to practice their religion.

The Shakers believed that simple living would make them happy and would bring them closer to God. They wore plain clothing and shared everything. They never married or had children. Men and women lived in separate houses.

The name "Shakers" came from the group's style of dancing. Dancing was an important part of Shaker religion. However, other people thought the Shaker dances were very strange.

"Simple Gifts" is a Shaker dance song written in 1848 that is still a popular folk song today.

2 *Listen to the song. Complete the song lyrics with the missing words from the box. Some words are used twice. Listen again if you need to.*

ashamed	delight	gained	~~simple~~
be	free	right	

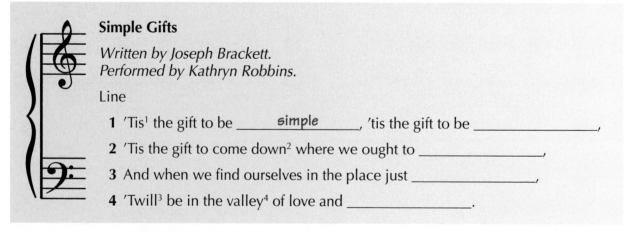

Simple Gifts

Written by Joseph Brackett.
Performed by Kathryn Robbins.

Line

1 'Tis[1] the gift to be _____simple_____, 'tis the gift to be _____,

2 'Tis the gift to come down[2] where we ought to _____,

3 And when we find ourselves in the place just _____,

4 'Twill[3] be in the valley[4] of love and _____.

---

[1]**'tis:** it is

[2]**come down:** stop at

[3]**'twill:** it will

[4]**valley:** a low area of land between two mountains

Refrain:

5 When true simplicity is _____,

6 To bow[5] and to bend we shan't[6] be _____.

7 To turn, turn will be our _____,

8 'Til[7] by turning, turning we come 'round _____.

(Repeat refrain)

3 CD2 *Listen again to the song. Many of the words have more than one meaning. What do you think these words mean in the song? Check (✓) all that apply.*

Meaning

Line 1: simple

a. not complicated   ○

b. without decoration   ○

c. easy to do   ○

Line 1: free

a. costs nothing   ○

b. not in prison   ○

c. not controlled by anyone or anything ○

Lines 3 and 8: right

a. opposite of *left*   ○

b. true   ○

c. the best choice   ○

4 *The song has several images (words that describe ideas). What do you think the images mean in the song?*

	MEANING
Lines 1–2: the gift	
Line 4: the valley of love and delight	
Lines 7–8: to turn	

---

[5]**bow:** to bend the top part of your body forward

[6]**shan't:** shall not, won't

[7]**'til:** until

◀ **STEP 1: Organize**

There are connections between the ideas in the Shaker song "Simple Gifts" and the lifestyle of the urban homesteaders. Work with a partner. Read the lines from the song. Then answer the questions.

LINES FROM "SIMPLE GIFTS"	QUESTIONS	ANSWERS FOR URBAN HOMESTEADERS
'Tis the gift to be simple.	1. What do the urban homesteaders do to lead a simple life?	they grow their own vegetables
'Tis the gift to be free.	2. In what ways are the urban homesteaders free? (What things are they free from?)	
'Tis the gift to come down where we ought to be.	3. Why is the inner city the place where the urban homesteaders want to be?	
'Twill be in the valley of love and delight.	4. What makes the urban homesteaders delighted (happy)?	

◀ **STEP 2: Synthesize**

Work with a new partner and compare your answers to the questions. Take turns reading the questions and responding by agreeing, disagreeing, or adding more information. Use the information from Step 1 and the useful language on the next page.

Example

STUDENT A: OK. Question 1 says, "What do the urban homesteaders do to lead a simple life?" Well . . . to lead a simple life the urban homesteaders grow their own vegetables.

STUDENT B: Right. They also don't use electricity.

Useful Language

Agreeing

- Right. They also . . .
- Yes, and they also . . .

Disagreeing

- I don't think . . . but . . .
- Actually, they . . .

 # 3 FOCUS ON SPEAKING

 **A VOCABULARY**

◖ **REVIEW**

1 *Work in a small group. Each group is given a name—Group A, Group B, etc. Choose five words or phrases from the box and write three clues for each one. (Everyone takes notes.)*

ashamed	gain	secondhand
consumption habits	homesteading	self-sufficient
convince	local economy	simplicity
delight	natural world	worth doing
fossil fuels	produce	

Example

Word: secondhand

Clues: not new, used, you can find it at a yard sale

2 *Meet in new groups. Each new group has one person from Group A, one from Group B, and so on. Take turns saying clues so the people in your new group can guess your words / phrases.*

Example

STUDENT A: OK. Here's the first clue: *not new*
STUDENT B: Old?
STUDENT A: No. Second clue: *used*
STUDENT C: Secondhand?
STUDENT A: Yes!

1 *Some people choose to simplify their lives in order to reduce stress. Read the article from a health magazine.*

Dealing with Stress: One Man's Story

I used to work as a manager for a big company. I made a lot of money, but I was always under a lot of stress. When I got home from work every day, I used to **unwind** by watching TV. I didn't want to talk to my wife or my kids. I never had time to take a vacation.

One day, I realized I was really unhappy. I knew I had to **get out of the rut** I was in, so I quit my job and started working part-time as a website designer. Now my life is totally

different. On weekends, I **take it easy** and don't rush around a lot. I spend more time with my children and **savor every moment** with them. The kids and I don't plan many activities. We just **go with the flow** and do whatever seems fun that day. The other day we went to a water park. We all had so much fun riding the 30-foot water slide. We **had a blast**.

I make less money now, but I'm enjoying life a lot more.

2 *Each idiom in the article above has a similar meaning to a common verb. Write the idiom in the blank next to its definition.*

enjoy

<u>to have a blast</u> : to have a fun and exciting experience

_____: to make an activity last as long as you can because you enjoy it

relax

_____: relax and stop worrying

_____: relax and don't do much

change

_____: change a situation that's been the same for a long time

_____: do something different without trying to control the situation

An analogy shows relationships between words. Below are four types of analogies that show different types of relationships.

ANALOGIES	EXAMPLES
Action : Object. Shows what action is used with an object	produce : vegetables A farmer produces vegetables in a garden.
Opposite. Shows two opposite things	go with the flow : make a plan Going with the flow is the opposite of making a plan.
Description. Shows what something is by describing it	homesteading : self-sufficient lifestyle Homesteading is a self-sufficient lifestyle.
Part : Whole. Shows a small part of something larger	plants : natural world Plants are part of the natural world.

Work with a partner. Make analogies for the words from the box. Try to make as many types of analogies as you can. You can use words more than once.

ashamed	go with the flow	secondhand
consumption habits	have a blast	self-sufficient
convince	homesteading	simplicity
delight	local economy	take it easy
fossil fuels	natural world	unwind
gain	produce	worth doing
get out of a rut	savor every moment	

1 *Take the quiz. Circle **True** or **False**.*

QUIZ: How simple is your life?

I buy *a lot of* things I don't really need.	True	False
I don't have *any* free time.	True	False
I'm under *a great deal of* stress.	True	False
I don't get *enough* sleep during the week.	True	False
I only have *a few* vacation days each year.	True	False

1. How many "true" answers do you have? Is your life simple?

2. Notice the words in italics. What kinds of words are these?

NOUNS AND QUANTIFIERS	
1. **Common nouns** refer to people, places, or things. **Abstract nouns** refer to ideas and feelings.	**People:** child, boss **Places:** city, farm **Things:** house, money **Abstract:** freedom, love, stress, time
2. Some nouns are **count nouns**, ideas you can count separately. Other nouns are **non-count nouns**, ideas that you cannot count separately. **NOTE:** Some nouns have both a **count** and a **non-count** meaning.	I have an **idea**. We have two **problems**. I'm under a great deal of **stress**. I didn't have enough **freedom**. We had a good **time** at the party. (count) time = an experience I don't have any **time** today. (non-count) time = availability
3. Use quantifiers **some, enough, a lot of**, and **any** with both **count nouns and non-count nouns**. Use **any** in questions and negative sentences.	There are **a lot of** reasons to simplify your life. He got into **a lot of** trouble. Do you have **any** worries? I don't have **any** fear.

4. Use *a few*, *several*, and *many* with **plural count nouns** in affirmative sentences.	There are **several** reasons to simplify your life.
Use *a little*, *a great deal of*, and *much* with **non-count nouns** in affirmative sentences.	You will have **a great deal of** happiness.
5. Use *many* with **count nouns** and *much* with **non-count nouns** in questions and negative sentences.	How **many** questions do you have? I don't have **many** questions. How **much** effort did you put in? I didn't put in **much** effort.

2 *Fill in each blank with the correct quantifier. Compare your answers with a partner's.*

1. a little / a few

If you have _____ extra time, take _____ minutes

to do something you enjoy, such as listening to music or reading a book.

_____ relaxation will help you.

2. many / a great deal of

_____ children today are too busy. Their days are filled with

school, homework, after-school classes, and sports events. They are under

_____ pressure and don't have _____

opportunities to play and have fun.

3. some / much

I wish I had _____ choice about my work schedule, but I don't.

I don't have _____ time to see my family on weekends.

4. any / enough

I used to work as a manager for a big company. I made _____

money, but I never had _____ fun. So I quit my job and started

working for myself. Now I have _____ freedom to do what I want.

5. how much / how many

_____ time do you spend at your computer each day?

_____ e-mails and text messages do you have to answer?

Sometimes we need to turn off our computers, walk away, and focus on

other things.

3 *Work with the same partner. Take turns asking and answering the questions. Use a quantifier in your answers.*

Example

STUDENT A: Do you spend <u>a lot of</u> time doing homework at night?
STUDENT B: Actually, I don't spend <u>much</u> time on homework.

1. Do you get _____ time to relax in the evenings?

2. How _____ hours of sleep do you usually get a night?

3. Do you have _____ opportunities to exercise during the week?

4. How _____ free time do you get on weekends?

5. Do you have _____ activities that you like to do just for fun?

6. Does your work require _____ energy?

C SPEAKING

◀ PRONUNCIATION: Noticing Rhythm

In language, rhythm is the pattern of stressed and unstressed syllables. To improve your English, you need to pay attention to and imitate the rhythm of English. Examples of content words are *garden, sell,* and *relaxing.* Content words are usually nouns, verbs, adjectives, and adverbs. In speaking, they have long stressed vowels. Grammar words like articles, pronouns, and prepositions are unstressed and harder to hear.

When most syllables in a sentence are stressed, the rhythm of the sentence sounds slower. When there are unstressed words and syllables, the rhythm sounds faster.

CD 2
(22) Listen to the conversations. How does the rhythm sound?

A: Lét's pláy póker.
B: We néed a déck of cárds.

A: Béth lóoks bád.
B: She's únder a lót of stréss.

1 CD 2 *Jazz chants have rhythmic patterns that repeat over and over. You can hear the*
(23) *pattern of stressed and unstressed beats easily in a chant. Listen to the chant on page 127 several times, tapping the rhythm with your finger or clapping your hands.*

Take Your Time

You're always in a hurry
You're always in a rush.

You always have to work.
You always have to go.

Where's the fire?
What's the rush?
Take your time.
Just relax.

You never take a break.
You're always under stress.
No time to read the paper.
No time to read a book.

Take a seat.
Close your eyes.
Take a breath.
What's the rush?

We miss your pretty face.
We want to see you more.
There's more to life than work, you know.
Relax and take a break.

2 Practice **Take Your Time.** *First, repeat the lines after your teacher. Then chant **Take Your Time** together. Next, divide into two groups. One group will chant the long lines; the other group will chant the short lines. Notice the rhythm of the chant.*

3 *Work with a partner and complete the lines below. In Student A's lines, most of the syllables are stressed, so the rhythm is slower. In Student B's lines, there are more unstressed syllables so the rhythm sounds faster. Practice saying the lines with your partner. Keep the stressed words long and loud.*

    1. STUDENT A: Cho looks thirsty.

        STUDENT B: Give him a ___glass___ of ___water___ .

    2. STUDENT A: Max isn't hungry.

        STUDENT B: He ate a _____ of _____ .

    3. STUDENT A: Young looks tired.

        STUDENT B: He needs a _____ of _____ .

    4. STUDENT A: Juan looks worried.

        STUDENT B: He's under a _____ of _____ .

    5. STUDENT A: Ann looks rested.

        STUDENT B: She got a _____ of _____ last night.

◀ FUNCTION: Descriptive Language

Descriptive language creates images, or pictures, in our minds. Using descriptive language can make your points more convincing and interesting to the listener. Descriptive language can include details about things you see, hear, smell, taste, or feel.

WAYS TO MAKE LANGUAGE DESCRIPTIVE	
Use adjectives and adverbs.	I enjoy walking **slowly** on the beach when the air is **fresh** and **cool**.
Add specific information.	**During the summer**, I enjoy walking slowly on the beach **near my house**.
Use words that appeal to the senses (sight, sound, touch, smell, taste).	I like to **feel** the hot sand under my feet and **hear** the waves crashing on the shore.

1 *People living a simple lifestyle often try to enjoy "simple pleasures," or activities that don't cost a lot and don't hurt the environment. Read the descriptions of some simple pleasures. Underline the descriptive language.*

    a. Every afternoon I drink a cup of tea. The cup feels warm in my hands. The tea tastes sweet and hot. I feel the hot steam on my face. The smell reminds me of home. I feel relaxed and comfortable.

    b. I love to play my piano. It's a beautiful instrument made of shiny black wood. The keys feel smooth and cool under my fingers. The music surrounds me— sometimes soft and light, sometimes loud and strong. When I play, I unwind and forget the stress of the day.

2 *Work in a group of three or four. Choose one of the simple pleasures from the list on page 129, or think of one of your own. Student A makes a statement about the activity. Student B repeats the statement and adds more description. Student C repeats Student B's statement and adds more description. Continue until everyone has taken a turn.*

Example

STUDENT A: I like sitting on the beach.
STUDENT B: I like sitting on the beach near my house.
STUDENT C: I like sitting on the beach near my house and listening to the crashing waves.
STUDENT D: I like sitting on the beach near my house, listening to the crashing waves, and feeling the warm sand under my feet.

Simple Pleasures

- hiking
- reading
- spending time with friends
- eating a good meal
- working in the garden
- playing _____ (musical instrument)
- your idea: _____

Choose another simple pleasure and repeat the activity.

◀ **PRODUCTION: Impromptu Presentation**

Impromptu presentations are talks that you give without much preparation. Making an impromptu presentation will challenge you to think quickly and will also give you practice talking in front of a group. In this activity, you will **make an impromptu presentation about simple pleasures**. Try to use the vocabulary, grammar, pronunciation, and descriptive language that you learned in the unit.*

Work in a group of five. Follow the steps.

Step 1: Look at the five categories of simple pleasures. Brainstorm a list of activities. Each student should suggest one activity he or she enjoys for each category. Take notes.

SIMPLE PLEASURES YOU DO . . .	ACTIVITIES
1. alone	*read a book,*
2. with one other person	*go dancing,*
3. with a group	*cook a meal with friends,*
4. in nature	
5. at home	

*For Alternative Speaking Topics, see page 130.

Step 2: Write each of the five categories on separate pieces of paper. Put the papers into a container. Each group member picks a piece of paper from the container. Look at the category you picked and choose one activity you listed in the chart for that category. Then each student takes four minutes to prepare a presentation on the activity. Use the outline as a guide.

Introduction: Tell the audience what activity you will talk about. ("Today I'd like to tell you about a simple pleasure that I enjoy....")

Body: Describe the activity in detail. You can include information about:

- how often you do the activity
- when and where you do it
- who is with you
- what you do
- a specific time you remember enjoying the activity
- other information

Conclusion: Explain why you enjoy the activity and why it is a simple pleasure. ("I enjoy _____ because . . .")

Step 3: Meet in your group. Take turns giving your presentation.

ALTERNATIVE SPEAKING TOPICS

Discuss one of the topics. Use the vocabulary and grammar from the unit.

1. Have you heard of anyone who has chosen to live a simple life? What has this person done to simplify his or her life? Why has he or she made this choice?

2. What are the advantages and disadvantages of living a self-sufficient lifestyle? What makes this lifestyle easier? What makes it harder?

RESEARCH TOPICS, see page 195.

Before You Say "I Do"

①FOCUS ON THE TOPIC

Ⓐ PREDICT

Discuss the questions with the class.

1. What's happening in the picture?

2. Look at the title of the unit. What happens before you say "I do"? What do you think this unit will be about?

Work in a small group. Read the quotations about marriage. After each quotation is a sentence that summarizes it. Circle the best answer to complete each statement.

1. "In almost every marriage, there is a selfish and an unselfish partner. A pattern begins and never changes, of one person always asking for something and the other person always giving something away."
   —Adapted from Iris Murdoch, British writer and philosopher (1919–1999)

   In most marriages, _____ can get what he or she wants.
   a. only one person
   b. both the husband and wife
   c. neither the husband nor the wife (no one)

2. "A man who is a good friend is likely to find a good wife because marriage is based on a talent for friendship."
   —Adapted from Friedrich Nietzsche, German philosopher (1844–1900)

   To have a happy marriage, a man must _____.
   a. have a good friend
   b. be a good friend to his wife
   c. be sure his wife has a good friend

3. "Keep your eyes wide open before marriage, and half shut afterwards."
   —Benjamin Franklin, American statesman and philosopher (1701–1790)

   Choose your husband or wife carefully, but _____ after marriage.
   a. ignore your spouse's[1] mistakes
   b. try to change your spouse
   c. don't look at your spouse

Discuss the quotations with the class. Do you agree or disagree with the writers? Why or why not?

C BACKGROUND AND VOCABULARY

1 🎧 CD 2 24 *Read and listen to information about a prenuptial[2] agreement.*

---

[1]**spouse:** husband or wife

[2]**prenuptial:** before marriage [pronounced: /prē-ˈnəp-shəl/]

A prenuptial agreement is a written agreement between two people who are going to get married. Most prenuptial agreements **concern** what will happen to a couple's money, property, or children if the marriage ends. It is used only if a problem **occurs** in the marriage and the couple decides to get divorced. However, some prenuptial agreements also describe how the husband and wife must act during the marriage. Steve and Karen Parsons made this type of agreement. They wrote a **contract** with rules for how they must behave in almost every part of their daily lives after they **tie the knot**.

Marriage Contract
Steve and Karen Parsons

1. Daily Habits
1.1 On weekdays, we will go to sleep by 11:00 P.M. and wake up by 6:00 A.M. On weekends, we will go to sleep by 1:00 A.M. and wake up by 10:00 A.M.
1.2 We will not drive over the speed limit and will always wear our seatbelts.
1.3 We will eat healthy food that is low in fat and sugar.

2. Household Chores
2.1 We will share the household chores. Steve will cook the meals and make repairs, and Karen will clean the house and take care of the garden.
2.2 We will both do the laundry. We will put the dirty clothes in the laundry bag, not on the floor. Steve will wash and dry the clothes, and Karen will fold them and put them away.
2.3 We will make a list of groceries every week. Karen will do the shopping. She will buy things on sale and not go over our **budget** for groceries.

3. Communication
3.1 If something **bothers** us, we will **open up** and talk about it immediately. We will not wait until it turns into a big problem.
3.2 If we disagree about something, we will **work out** the problem and find a compromise.
3.3 We promise to respect each other and not to criticize each other's **quirks** or habits.

4. Children
4.1 We will wait for two years before we have a child. We will have two children.
4.2 After our first child is born, the partner who makes less money will quit his or her job and stay home with the child. The partner who makes more money will become the **breadwinner** for the family.

We both understand our partner's **expectations** for how we will behave in our marriage. We can both **check up on** each other to make sure our partner is following the rules.

Signed,

Steve Parsons **Karen Parsons**

2 *Match the words on the left with the definitions on the right.*

_____ **1.** concern   **a.** happen

_____ **2.** occur   **b.** solve

_____ **3.** contract   **c.** the person who earns money to support the family

_____ **4.** tie the knot   **d.** annoy

_____ **5.** budget   **e.** make sure someone is doing something correctly

_____ **6.** bother   **f.** a legal agreement between two people

_____ **7.** open up   **g.** to say what you really think

_____ **8.** work out   **h.** a strange or unusual habit

_____ **9.** quirk   **i.** to be about

_____ **10.** breadwinner   **j.** a belief or hope that something will happen

_____ **11.** expectation   **k.** a plan for how to spend money

_____ **12.** check up on   **l.** get married

②FOCUS ON LISTENING

Ⓐ LISTENING ONE: A Prenuptial Agreement

CD 2
25
You will hear an interview with Steve and Karen Parsons about their prenuptial agreement. Listen to the beginning of the interview. Then read some questions the reporter will ask Steve and Karen later in the interview. How do you think they will answer the questions? Write your predictions below.

1. "So, I'd like to start off by asking you what *everybody* is probably wondering. . . . Why did you decide to write this agreement?"

   Predicted answer: _____

2. "I'm curious . . . Do you spend a lot of time checking up on each other to see if the rules are being followed?"

   Predicted answer: _____

3. "Do you think other couples should follow your example and write marriage contracts of their own?"

   Predicted answer: _____

◗ LISTEN FOR MAIN IDEAS

🎵 CD 2
26 *Listen to the interview. Steve and Karen are discussing several problems that married people have. Put a check (✓) next to the four problems that are mentioned in the interview.*

_____ **1.** Different expectations

_____ **2.** Problems with other family members

_____ **3.** Not respecting each other's quirks

_____ **4.** Arguments about pets

_____ **5.** Not talking about what each person wants

_____ **6.** Disagreements about money

_____ **7.** Relationships with other men or women

◗ LISTEN FOR DETAILS

🎵 CD 2
27 *Listen again. Decide if each statement is true or false. Write **T** (true) or **F** (false).*

_____ **1.** Steve and Karen have a five-page prenuptial agreement.

_____ **2.** Both Steve and Karen have been married before.

_____ **3.** It bothered Steve when his ex-wife left her clothes lying on the floor.

_____ **4.** Karen thinks that working out a compromise is more romantic than flowers and candy.

_____ **5.** Karen says that the prenuptial agreement is like a business contract.

_____ **6.** Karen and Steve argue about their budget.

_____ **7.** Steve and Karen feel that they spend the same amount of time arguing as other couples do.

_____ **8.** Steve and Karen agree about all the rules in the prenuptial agreement.

_____ **9.** Steve and Karen feel that a prenuptial agreement could be useful for other couples.

◖ MAKE INFERENCES

*Listen to three excerpts from the interview. Then read the summaries of the quotations from Section IB. Would Steve and Karen agree with the ideas in each summary? Check (✓) **Yes** or **No**. Write down words or phrases from the listening that support your answer.*

⟨CD2 28⟩ Excerpt One

The quote by Benjamin Franklin says that you should choose your spouse carefully, but ignore his or her mistakes after marriage.

Would Steve and Karen agree with this idea?   ◯ Yes   ◯ No

Words or phrases to support your answer: _____

⟨CD2 29⟩ Excerpt Two

The quote by Iris Murdoch says that in most marriages only one person can get what he or she wants.

Would Steve and Karen agree with this idea?   ◯ Yes   ◯ No

Words or phrases to support your answer: _____

⟨CD2 30⟩ Excerpt Three

The quote by Friedrich Nietzsche says that to have a happy marriage, a man must be a good friend to his wife.

Would Steve and Karen agree with this idea?   ◯ Yes   ◯ No

Words or phrases to support your answer: _____

Compare your answers in a small group. Why would Steve and Karen agree or disagree with each quote? Give examples from the listening to explain your answer.

◖ EXPRESS OPINIONS

Discuss the questions in a small group.

1. Do you agree or disagree with Steve and Karen's opinions about marriage? Work individually to make a list of the ideas that you agree and disagree with. Then discuss your ideas.

2. What would you say if your fiancé / fiancée[1] asked you to write a prenuptial agreement like Steve and Karen's?

---

[1]**fiancé / fiancée:** the man / woman you are going to marry

B LISTENING TWO: Reactions to the Prenuptial Agreement

CD 2 *Listen to different people calling the talk show to share their reactions to Steve and*
31 *Karen's prenuptial agreement. Do they think the agreement is a good idea or a bad*
idea? Check (✓) the appropriate column according to each caller's opinion. Then
match each caller with the reason for his or her opinion. Write the letter of the
reason in the chart. One reason isn't mentioned in the listening.

	GOOD IDEA	BAD IDEA	REASON
Caller 1			
Caller 2			
Caller 3			
Caller 4			
Caller 5			

REASONS (match with speakers)

a. Couples learn to open up about their problems.

b. It helps couples think carefully before they marry.

c. Each spouse has to follow a budget.

d. Not romantic

e. Too many details

f. Not legal

C INTEGRATE LISTENINGS ONE AND TWO

◀ **STEP 1: Organize**

Work with a partner. Combine the ideas in Listenings One and Two to write a list of
*arguments **for** and **against** prenuptial agreements. Then note an example to explain*
each reason.

ARGUMENTS FOR PRENUPTIAL AGREEMENTS	EXAMPLES

(continued on next page)

ARGUMENTS *AGAINST* PRENUPTIAL AGREEMENTS	EXAMPLES

◀ **STEP 2: Synthesize**

Work with a partner. Debate the topic of prenuptial agreements. One partner takes the pro position (in favor) and the other partner takes the con position (against). Use the information from Step 1 to support your position.

Useful Language

- I support / oppose prenuptial agreements because . . .
- I'm for / against . . .
- I think / don't think . . .
- For example, . . .

Switch partners and repeat the debate, with each person taking the opposite side.

③ FOCUS ON SPEAKING

Ⓐ VOCABULARY

◀ **REVIEW**

1 *Make words from the scrambled letters. Write one letter in each square. Don't worry yet about the numbers below the boxes. You will use them in the next exercise.*

1. Most arguments between my wife and me NCCORNE money.

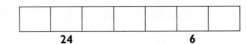

2. Problems often COCUR in a marriage when the husband and wife don't communicate well.

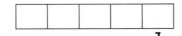

3. When my wife and I have a problem, we ROKW TUO a solution we both agree on.

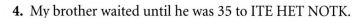

	33		14			

4. My brother waited until he was 35 to ITE HET NOTK.

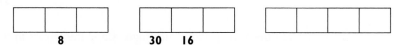

	8			30	16				

5. We made a BUTDEG so we don't spend too much money.

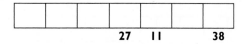

		39	10	25	

6. It really BEORTHS me when my husband leaves dirty dishes in the sink.

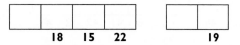

			27	11		38

7. I trust my wife, so I can really NOEP PU and tell her how I feel.

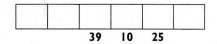

	18	15	22		19

8. Our marriage CATTOCNR states that if we have children, they will have the same last name as their mother.

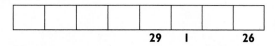

			29	1		26	

9. Traditionally, a husband is the DREWEBRANNI for the family.

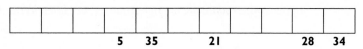

	5	35		21			28	34		

10. My parents and I have different PAXTOETEINSC about whom I will marry.

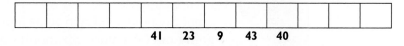

	41	23	9	43	40						

11. Each person should treat his or her PUOSES with love and respect.

	42	12			

12. My husband is very RNMAITOC. He likes to buy flowers and cards for me.

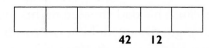

32		4	13		20		

13. Some LOESUPC live together before they get married.

				2	31	36

14. Steve and Karen Parsons have an unusual PLTAUPENRI agreement.

								37	17	3

2 *Figure out the saying about marriage. Copy the letters in the numbered squares from Exercise 1 to the squares below with the same numbers.*

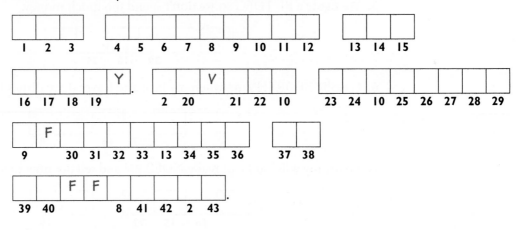

—Anonymous

Discuss with the class whether you agree with this saying.

(EXPAND

Read the letter to a newspaper advice column. Look at the boldfaced phrases that describe actions. Discuss the meanings you don't know with a partner. Then decide whether the action happens when someone is single, married, or either. Write the action in the appropriate box.

Ask Gabby

Dear Gabby,
I met my boyfriend two years ago, and we have been **going out** ever since. Six months ago, we started **living together**. Now I think I'm ready to **tie the knot**, but he still hasn't **proposed**. I think he's nervous about it because his dad **cheated on** his mom, and his parents **separated** and later **got divorced**. I know he's afraid, but I want to **be in a relationship** that leads to marriage. I can't wait forever, so I'm thinking of **breaking up with him**. What should I do? I don't really want to **be single** again.
-Amy H.

HAPPENS WHEN SOMEONE IS ...		
single	**married**	**either**
tie the knot		

◖ **CREATE**

Work in a small group to create a role play. Follow the steps.

1. Write each word or phrase from the word box on a small piece of paper. Fold the papers and mix them together in a container.

be in a relationship	contract	prenuptial
be single	couple	propose
bother	expectations	romantic
breadwinner	get divorced	separate
break up with someone	go out	spouse
budget	live together	tie the knot
cheat on	open up	work out

2. Pick four pieces of paper and read them as a group. Do not show them to the class.

3. Choose a situation from the list. As a group, create a role play about the situation. In your role play, use the four vocabulary words you picked.

Situations
- Parents and other family members are talking to their son or daughter about his or her plans for marriage.
- Friends are discussing what kind of spouse they want.
- A couple is discussing their roles in their relationship (who will earn money, take care of children, cook, clean, etc.).
- Family members are talking about a couple that is breaking up or getting a divorce.
- [Make up a situation]

4. Practice the role play and then perform it for the class.

As you watch the role plays by the other groups, listen carefully for the four vocabulary words they use. Write them down. When the role play is finished, check to see if your words match the pieces of paper that the performers picked.

1 *Read the conversation. Look at the boldfaced words and answer the questions.*

KAISA: How's married life?

NORIKO: It's **as wonderful as** living together, but different.

KAISA: How so?

NORIKO: Well, I think our relationship is **stronger**. We're **less worried** about breaking up, and we're **more careful** about saving money.

KAISA: Sounds like married life is **better than** being single.

NORIKO: It is.

1. Which phrase expresses the idea that two things are *equal*?

2. Which phrase(s) express the idea of *more*? Which expresses the idea of *less*?

COMPARATIVES AND EQUATIVES	
1. Use **equatives** to express the idea of "equal": • Use *as + adjective + as*.	I have been married **as long as** my brother.
2. Use **comparative adjectives** to express the idea of "more": • Use **adjective + -er + than** with one-syllable adjectives. • If an adjective ends in **-y**, change the **-y** to **-i** and add **-er + than**. • Use *more + adjective + than* with adjectives that have two or more syllables.	My brother has been married **longer than** I have. My second marriage is **happier than** my first. As a gift, flowers are **more romantic than** books.
3. Use comparatives to express the idea of "less": • Use *less + adjective + than*. • Use *not as + adjective + as*. With one-syllable adjectives, *not as . . . as* is more common than *less . . . than*.	My wife is **less patient than** I am. Our marriage is **not as strong as** it used to be.
4. There are some irregular **comparative** forms.	Adjective Comparative bad worse good better
5. It's not necessary to mention both parts of the comparison when the meaning is clear.	My brother has been married **longer**. Flowers are **more romantic**.

2 *Fill in the blanks with comparatives and equatives. The "+" sign means more. The "–" sign means less. The "=" sign means equal.*

KAISA: I'm **(1.)** _____less interested_____ (interested –) than you in settling down.

I like my freedom too much.

NORIKO: I guess my life is not **(2.)** _____ (free –). It's

(3.) _____ (easy +) for Greg to plan if he knows what

I'm doing. So I let him know if I'm going to be at work

(4.) _____ (late +) than usual.

KAISA: See. That's what I mean. I'm **(5.)** _____ (happy +) when I

can come and go as I please.

NORIKO: But for me, being single is way **(6.)** _____ (stressful +) than

being married. It's a lot **(7.)** _____ (difficult +) to make

decisions about important stuff if you don't have someone to talk to.

I like married life a lot **(8.)** _____ (good +).

KAISA: Well, I'm glad it's working for you. Maybe one day I'll find the right guy,

get married, and be **(9.)** _____ (happy =) you.

NORIKO: Maybe.

3 *Work in a small group. Discuss the following topic: "Is it better to be married or single? Why?" Use the adjectives from the box and add your own.*

bad	difficult	happy	serious
busy	easy	lonely	stressful
comfortable	free	responsible	strong
concerned	good	romantic	worried

Example

STUDENT A: I think it's *more difficult* to be single than to be married. If you're
single, you're always looking for someone.

STUDENT B: That's true. I think married people aren't *as lonely as* single people.

STUDENT C: Not necessarily. . . .

◀ PRONUNCIATION: Contrastive Stress

When we want to emphasize a difference, we stress the words that show the difference. This kind of emphasis is called contrastive stress. We also use contrastive stress to show that some information is correct and other information is incorrect.

CD 2
32 Listen to the sentences. Note how the underlined words are emphasized.

I do the <u>laundry</u>, and <u>Steve</u> does the <u>dishes</u>.

I want to hear <u>good</u> news, <u>not</u> <u>bad</u> news.

CONTRASTIVE STRESS	
Emphasize words that show a contrast (a difference).	My **wife drives** to work, and **I** take the **bus**.
Emphasize words that show correct and incorrect information.	Your appointment is **tomorrow, not today**.
To emphasize a word, say the word: • on a high pitch (tone). • louder. • longer.	Tell me the **good** news (not the bad news). Tell me the **GOOD** news. Tell me the **g o o o d** news.

1 CD 2 *Listen to the sentences. Underline the word that is emphasized. Then circle **a** or **b*** **33** *to choose the meaning of the sentence.*

1. <u>Karen</u> will do the grocery shopping.
   - **(a.)** not Steve
   - **b.** not the laundry

2. Karen will always use a shopping list.
   - **a.** not Steve
   - **b.** not sometimes

3. Nothing will be left on the floor in the bedroom.
   - **a.** not the table
   - **b.** not the living room

4. On weekdays, we will go to bed at 11:00 P.M.
   - **a.** not weekends
   - **b.** not at 9:00 P.M.

5. We will wait three years before buying a house.
   - **a.** not two years
   - **b.** not a car

6. Karen will make a list of groceries every week.

   a. not Steve   **b.** not whenever we remember

7. We will spend at least 15 minutes a day talking with each other.

   a. not less than 15 minutes   **b.** not our relatives

8. Steve will figure out directions before we start a trip.

   a. not Karen   **b.** not after we start

9. We will eat healthy food that's low in fat and sugar.

   a. not junk food   **b.** both fat and sugar

10. We will update this agreement every year.

   a. not our lawyers   **b.** not every two years

2 *Work with a partner. Student A says the sentences from Exercise 1, using word stress to show either meaning **a** or meaning **b**. Student B listens and guesses the meaning of the sentences. Then switch roles and repeat.*

Example

Karen will do <u>the grocery shopping</u>.

a. not Steve   **b.** not the laundry

STUDENT A: Karen will do **the grocery shopping**.
STUDENT B: That means "not the laundry," right?
STUDENT A: Yes.

3 *Work with a partner. Each of the following sentences has two sets of words that are contrasted with each other. Read the sentences and circle the first set of words that are contrasted. Then underline the second set. Take turns reading the sentences aloud, using contrastive stress.*

1. (Steve's) been married <u>twice</u>, and (Karen's) been married <u>once</u>.

2. Many of the rules deal with money; only a few deal with other situations.

3. Steve takes care of the car and Karen does the housework.

4. Getting married is easy, but living together afterward is more difficult.

5. On weekends, Karen gets up early and Steve gets up late.

6. When it comes to food, Steve likes Japanese and Karen likes Mexican.

7. One couple got marriage counseling, while the other couple got a divorce.

8. Most couples make verbal agreements; only a few want written agreements.

◖ FUNCTION: Transitions in Oral Presentations

We use transitions to make oral presentations clear. Transitions can be used to introduce main ideas and supporting points.

A. Transitions for Introducing Main Ideas

1 *Read the introductions to oral presentations. Underline the main idea that will be discussed in each presentation. Then circle the transitions used to introduce the main idea. Report your answers to the class.*

1. Some people think that prenuptial agreements are a crazy idea, but in my opinion they can help couples think about the realities of marriage. Today I'd like to talk about the advantages of prenuptial agreements.

2. There's a new trend in love and marriage: prenuptial agreements. You may have heard of them, but do you really know what they are? I'm going to define prenuptial agreements and explain why they're becoming popular.

3. Prenuptial agreements may seem like a good idea for Hollywood movie stars. They go through two or three marriages in a lifetime. But for regular people like you and me, these contracts are a mistake. The question that I will discuss today is: "What's the problem with prenuptial agreements?"

B. Transitions for Introducing Supporting Points

2 *Read the lists of transitions for introducing supporting points.*

TRANSITIONS FOR INTRODUCING SUPPORTING POINTS	
Points of Equal Importance	**Points from Most to Least Important**
One reason is . . .	The most important reason is . . .
Another reason is . . .	Another important reason is . . .
And last but not least[1] . . .	A final reason is . . .

---

[1] **last but not least:** the last point is not less important than the others

3 Look at the presentation outlines. Decide whether the supporting points are equally *important or not. Fill in the blanks with transitions for introducing the main idea and the supporting points. Read your answers to a partner.*

A. Main idea: _____ the benefits of prenuptial agreements.

    Supporting point 1: _____ it encourages couples to think carefully before they get married.

    Supporting point 2: _____ it helps couples talk about things that are important to them.

    Supporting point 3: _____ it makes expectations clearer.

B. Main idea: _____: "What is wrong with prenuptial agreements?"

    Supporting point 1: _____ it shows that couples don't trust each other.

    Supporting point 2: _____ it doesn't allow people to change and grow.

    Supporting point 3: _____ it makes couples think about divorce before they even get married.

◖ **PRODUCTION: Oral Presentation**

In this activity, you will **give a 3–5-minute presentation on a controversial topic related to marriage**. Try to use the vocabulary, grammar, pronunciation, and transitions for introducing main ideas and supporting points that you learned in the unit.*

Follow the steps.

Step 1: Choose a topic for your presentation. You may choose one of the following topics or think of your own topic.

- living together before marriage
- the rights of unmarried couples
- using dating services to find a spouse (Internet sites, personal ads, speed dating)
- arranged marriages vs. love marriages
- mixed marriages (religion, age, language, culture, race)

---

*For Alternative Speaking Topics, see page 149.

- types of families (blended[1], single parent)
- living situations in marriage (long-distance marriages, living with relatives)
- divorce
- Other: _____

Write a sentence stating your opinion about the topic: _____

_____

Example

Topic: Prenuptial Agreements

Opinion: I think prenuptial agreements are a good way to prepare for marriage.

Step 2: Plan your presentation using the outline. Practice giving your presentation to a friend or in front of a mirror.

Introduction (1/2 to 1 minute)

- Introduce the topic
- Give background information
- State your opinion

Body (2–3 minutes)

Give two or three reasons for your opinion

- State each reason
- Explain each reason using details and examples

Conclusion (1/2 minute)

- Restate your opinion
- Make a concluding statement (e.g., summary of reasons, prediction for the future, quotation, question)

Step 3: Give your presentation to the class. When presenting, look at the audience and use your outline as a guide. Speak loudly and clearly.

---

[1]**blended family:** a family formed when two families are joined by marriage; a stepfamily

ALTERNATIVE SPEAKING TOPICS

Look at the graph and discuss the topics. Use the vocabulary and grammar from the unit.

What Makes a Marriage Work?

Percent saying each is very important for a successful marriage

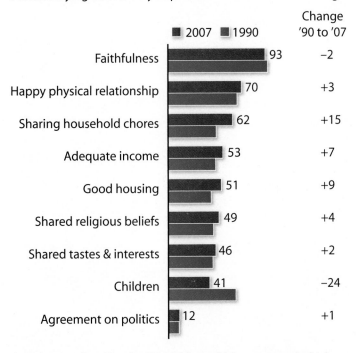

	2007	Change '90 to '07
Faithfulness	93	−2
Happy physical relationship	70	+3
Sharing household chores	62	+15
Adequate income	53	+7
Good housing	51	+9
Shared religious beliefs	49	+4
Shared tastes & interests	46	+2
Children	41	−24
Agreement on politics	12	+1

Question wording: Here is a list of things which some people think make for a successful marriage. Please tell me, for each one, whether you think it is very important, rather important, or not very important.

Source: 1990 survey by World Values; 2007 survey by Pew Research Center.

http://pewresearch.org/pbs/526/marriage-parenthood

1. According to the survey, what do Americans feel is most important for a successful marriage? What is least important?

2. How do you think people in your country would answer the questions?

3. In your opinion, what two things listed on the chart are most important for a successful marriage? What two are least important?

RESEARCH TOPICS, see page 195.

Personal Carbon Footprint

1 FOCUS ON THE TOPIC

A PREDICT

Look at the picture and discuss the questions with the class.

1. Carbon dioxide (CO_2) gas is made by burning fuel such as gasoline, diesel, oil, coal, or wood. What do you think are the effects of too much CO_2 in the air?

2. What do you think a *personal carbon footprint* is?

A *footprint* is a mark left by a foot. It can also describe the effect that a person has on the environment. Your *personal carbon footprint* is the amount of carbon dioxide (CO_2) that you put into the air when you use electricity, drive a car, and heat or cool your house.

1 *Is your personal carbon footprint big or little? Complete the survey to find out. Circle the number in the column that best describes your lifestyle.*

PERSONAL CARBON FOOTPRINT SURVEY			
	Often	Sometimes	Never
1. Do you drive a car more than 20 minutes a day?	2	1	0
2. Do you fly in a plane more than 7 hours a year?	2	1	0
3. Do you bike, walk, or take public transportation?	0	1	2
4. Do you turn off lights and appliances when you are not using them?	0	1	2
5. Do you use appliances (TVs, computers, clothes driers, refrigerators, etc.) that save energy?	0	1	2
6. Do you heat your house?	2	1	0
7. Do you use air-conditioning to cool your house?	2	1	0
8. Do you buy food that is grown close to your home?	0	1	2
Total			

If you scored:

0–5 You have a small carbon footprint.
5–10 You have a medium carbon footprint.
11–16 You have a large carbon footprint.

2 *Discuss your answers in a small group. How large is your personal carbon footprint? Are you surprised? Why or why not?*

C BACKGROUND AND VOCABULARY

1 CD 2 **34** *Read and listen to the explanation of global warming.*

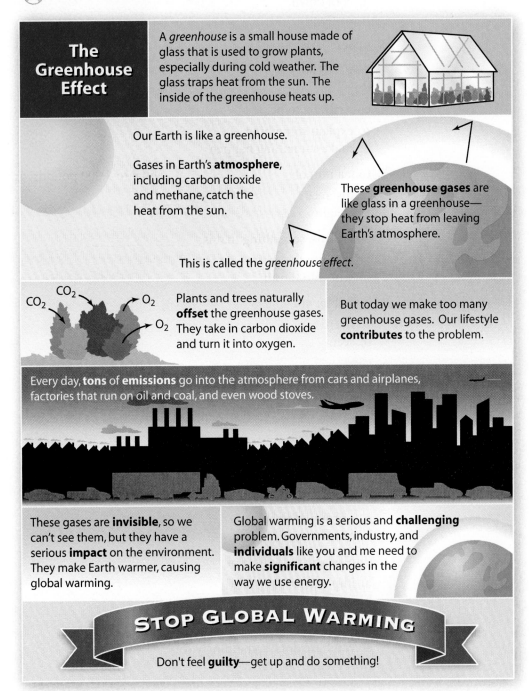

The Greenhouse Effect

A *greenhouse* is a small house made of glass that is used to grow plants, especially during cold weather. The glass traps heat from the sun. The inside of the greenhouse heats up.

Our Earth is like a greenhouse.

Gases in Earth's **atmosphere**, including carbon dioxide and methane, catch the heat from the sun.

These **greenhouse gases** are like glass in a greenhouse— they stop heat from leaving Earth's atmosphere.

This is called the *greenhouse effect*.

CO_2 CO_2 O_2 O_2

Plants and trees naturally **offset** the greenhouse gases. They take in carbon dioxide and turn it into oxygen.

But today we make too many greenhouse gases. Our lifestyle **contributes** to the problem.

Every day, **tons** of **emissions** go into the atmosphere from cars and airplanes, factories that run on oil and coal, and even wood stoves.

These gases are **invisible**, so we can't see them, but they have a serious **impact** on the environment. They make Earth warmer, causing global warming.

Global warming is a serious and **challenging** problem. Governments, industry, and **individuals** like you and me need to make **significant** changes in the way we use energy.

STOP GLOBAL WARMING

Don't feel **guilty**—get up and do something!

2 *Circle the correct word or phrase to complete each definition.*

1. **atmosphere:** the mixture of gases that _____
   a. is made by cars and trucks
   b. surround the earth

2. **greenhouse gases:** gases that cause the earth to _____
   a. cool down
   b. heat up

3. **offset:** have the _____ effect as something else
   a. opposite
   b. same

4. **contribute:** to help _____
   a. explain something
   b. make something happen

5. **ton:** a unit of _____ equal to 2,000 pounds, or 0.907 metric tons
   a. distance
   b. weight

6. **emissions:** something that is _____
   a. put into the earth
   b. sent into the air

7. **invisible:** not able to be _____
   a. heard
   b. seen

8. **impact:** the _____ of an event or situation
   a. effect
   b. cause

9. **challenging:** _____ to do
   a. difficult
   b. easy

10. **individual:** _____
    a. a group of people
    b. one person

11. **significant:** noticeable or _____
    a. important
    b. difficult

12. **guilty:** ashamed or sad because _____
    a. you have done something wrong
    b. someone has hurt you

②FOCUS ON LISTENING

Ⓐ LISTENING ONE: Personal Carbon Footprint

ᶜᴰ² ③⑤ *Listen to an excerpt from a radio report. What will the report be about? Circle your predictions.*

a. the amount of CO_2 emissions in the world today

b. ways to reduce CO_2 emissions

c. problems caused by CO_2 emissions

◖LISTEN FOR MAIN IDEAS

ᶜᴰ² ③⑥ *Listen to the report. Circle the best answer to complete each statement.*

1. Ellen Schoenfeld-Beeks is a _____ who paid to offset her carbon footprint.
   a. homeowner   **b.** business owner   **c.** government official

2. Anton Finelli started a website for _____ to pay to offset their carbon emissions.
   a. governments   **b.** businesses   **c.** individuals

3. Rich Rosenzweig thinks most _____ won't pay to offset their carbon emissions.
   a. businesses   **b.** individuals   **c.** governments

◖LISTEN FOR DETAILS

ᶜᴰ² ③⑦ *Listen to the report again. Then read each statement and decide if it is true or false. Write **T** (true) or **F** (false).*

1. Ellen Schoenfeld-Beeks . . .

   _____ **a.** sees many things around the house that emit carbon dioxide.

   _____ **b.** uses solar power to heat her house.

   _____ **c.** makes 20 tons of carbon dioxide per year.

2. Anton Finelli . . .

   _____ **a.** believes people should feel guilty for increasing global warming.

   _____ **b.** thinks that millions of individual payments can help the environment.

   _____ **c.** uses the money to collect methane from landfills and plant trees.

(continued on next page)

3. Rich Rosenzweig . . .

_____ **a.** collects money from businesses to reduce carbon emissions.

_____ **b.** thinks that Finelli's business will be successful.

_____ **c.** makes payments to Finelli's Web site.

4. Ellen Schoenfeld-Beeks . . .

_____ **a.** plans to increase her payments to offset carbon emissions.

_____ **b.** feels better because she's helping the environment.

_____ **c.** has stopped using her wood stove.

◖ **MAKE INFERENCES**

Listen to excerpts from the report. What would each speaker think about the following statements? If the speaker would agree with the statement, write **agree** in the box. If the speaker would disagree, write **disagree**. If there isn't enough information to know, leave the box blank.

	CD 2 38 **EXCERPT 1** _FINELLI_	CD 2 39 **EXCERPT 2** _ROSENZWEIG_	CD 2 40 **EXCERPT 3** _SCHOENFELD-BEEKS_
1. Paying to offset carbon emissions will help stop global warming.			
2. Businesses can make money by charging individuals to offset their carbon emissions.			
3. Individual people should do something to stop global warming.			

Work with a partner. Explain your answers with information from the report.

◖ EXPRESS OPINIONS

Work in a small group. Discuss your opinions using the sentence starters.

1. I would / wouldn't pay to offset my personal carbon footprint because . . .

2. Individuals can help stop global warming by . . .

B | **LISTENING TWO: A Call to Action**

You will hear a speech from an environmental rally to stop global warming.

1 CD 2 🔘41 *Listen to the speech. Label the percentages in the graph with the source of CO_2 emissions.*

   a. making electricity

   b. transportation

   c. industry (businesses and factories)

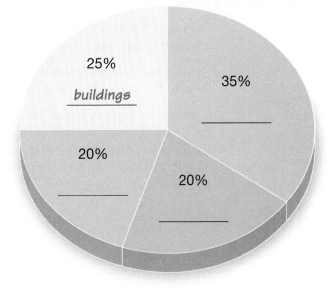

25%
buildings

35%
_____

20%
_____

20%
_____

2 *What is the main point the speaker is trying to make? Circle the correct answer.*

a. Factories and businesses produce a lot of pollution.

b. Government and industry need to do more to reduce carbon emissions.

c. Individuals should do more to reduce their personal carbon footprints.

C (INTEGRATE LISTENINGS ONE AND TWO

(STEP 1: Organize

Complete the chart with information from Listenings One and Two.

	RADIO REPORT	SPEECH AT A RALLY
Group A What can individuals do to stop climate change?		
Group B What can government and industry do to stop climate change?		

(STEP 2: Synthesize

Divide into two groups to create a fluency line. Use the information from Step 1 to answer the questions.

Work in two groups, A and B. Each group stands in a line so that Group A students are standing opposite Group B students.

Students in Group A begin. Ask your partner (standing opposite you in Group B) the Group A question. Your partner responds. When your teacher says, "Switch," students in Group A move to the next partner in line and ask the same question. Repeat again with a new partner. Now change roles. Group B asks and Group A answers.

3 FOCUS ON SPEAKING

A VOCABULARY

◖ REVIEW

Fill in the blanks with the correct words.

atmosphere	challenging	greenhouse gases	individuals

1. Carbon dioxide and methane are _____.

2. The _____ is made up of a mixture of gases that surround the Earth.

3. This problem is _____, so we must work hard to find a solution.

4. _____ can reduce their own carbon footprints.

invisible	pollution	significant	tons

5. We can't see carbon dioxide. It is _____.

6. Every time I drive my big car I add _____ to the air.

7. It's hard to know the exact amount of carbon that a car produces, but we know that it's many _____ per year.

8. Climate change is a _____ problem. Many scientists think that it is the most important environmental problem today.

(continued on next page)

contribute	emissions	impact	offset

9. Every year I plant three trees to _____ the carbon dioxide my car produces.

10. We are beginning to see some of the effects of global warming, but we won't know the _____ of climate change on the environment for many years.

11. Wood stoves add some greenhouse gases to the air, but cars and factories _____ even more.

12. _____ from factories increase greenhouse gases.

◖ EXPAND

1 *Complete the chart with the missing word forms. Use a dictionary to help you.*

NOUN	VERB	ADJECTIVE
atmosphere	—	atmospheric
challenge		challenging
	contribute	—
emissions		—
energy	—	
impact		—
	—	individual
industry	—	
		polluted
product		

2 *Look at the pairs of sentences. Each pair has a different form of the same word (for example, **atmosphere**, **atmospheric**). Choose the correct word form to complete each sentence.*

1. Greenhouse gases trap heat in the ____atmosphere____.

   Scientists are doing ____atmospheric____ research to understand the effects of climate change.

2. Climate change is caused by carbon _____ from burning coal, oil, and natural gas.

   Wood stoves also _____ carbon dioxide.

3. Stopping climate change is a _____ problem.

   Many scientists say it's the biggest _____ we face today.

4. Emissions from cars and trucks _____ to the greenhouse effect.

   I gave a small _____ to an environmental group to help stop climate change.

5. _____ needs to do more to stop global warming.

   The air is polluted because we live in an _____ area.

6. Factories, cars, and trucks _____ the air.

   The air in Los Angeles and Mexico City has a lot of _____.

7. What is your _____ carbon footprint?

   Anton Finelli collects donations from many _____.

8. We _____ most of our electricity by burning coal.

   Consumers want to buy more _____ that save energy and lower emissions.

9. Reducing the number of cars on the road will have a big _____ on climate change.

   Carbon emissions have _____ the environment and caused global warming.

10. We need to reduce the amount of _____ we use.

    The _____ crowd marched down the street, chanting and singing, to protest global warming.

◖ CREATE

Work in a small group. Each student reads one of the statements aloud. The other students agree or disagree and explain why. Use the vocabulary from the box in your answers.

atmosphere	impact
challenge / challenging	individual(s)
contribution / contribute	industry / industrial
emissions / emit	offset
energy / energetic	pollute / pollution / polluted
fossil fuel	product / produce
greenhouse gases	significant

1. Government can have a bigger impact on global warming than individuals.

2. Industries should contribute 20 percent of their money to offset their emissions.

3. To reduce greenhouse gases, more countries should get their energy from nuclear power.

4. Countries that produce the most greenhouse gases should take the most responsibility for solving the problem of global warming.

5. Climate change is the most significant problem the world is facing today.

B GRAMMAR: Modals of Necessity

1 *Read the radio interview with an environmental activist. Then answer the questions.*

HOST: What **do** individuals **have to** do to reduce their personal carbon footprint?

ACTIVIST: Well, we all **have to** drive less. We also need better public transportation, so that we **don't have to** take our cars everywhere.

HOST: What else?

ACTIVIST: Everyone **must** work together. We can't solve this problem alone. And we **must not** wait too long to make these changes—or else our climate will change forever.

1. What is the difference between *have to* and *must*?

2. What is the difference between *doesn't have to* and *must not*?

MODALS OF NECESSITY

1. Use *have to* and *must* to tell when something is necessary.	
Have to is usually used in conversation and informal writing.	We **have to** find ways to reduce emissions.
Must is used most often in writing.	We **must** stop global warming.
NOTE: *Must* is stronger than *have to*.	
2. Use *have to* for all tenses.	We **have to** make changes today. We **had to** start making changes years ago. We'll **have to** make more changes in the future.
Use *must* only for present and future tenses.	We **must** make changes today. We **must** make more changes in the future.
3. Use *have to* for questions.	What **do** individuals **have to** do? **Do** they **have to** stop driving?
NOTE: *Must* is almost never used in questions.	
4. Use *don't / doesn't have to* when something is not necessary (when there is a choice).	We **don't have to** drive everywhere.
Use *must not* when something is prohibited (when there is no choice).	We **must not / can't** wait too long to make changes.
NOTE: In spoken English, *can't* is often used instead of *must not*.	

2 *Read the rest of the interview with the environmental activist. Circle the best modal of necessity for each question.*

HOST: What do businesses have to do to reduce emissions?

ACTIVIST: First of all, business leaders (**1.**) *must / don't have to* find new ways to reduce emissions from industry.

HOST: Will that cost a lot?

ACTIVIST: Reducing emissions (**2.**) *can't / doesn't have to* be expensive. In fact, businesses often save money.

HOST: How can our government help?

ACTIVIST: Governments (**3.**) *don't have to / must not* ignore the emissions problem. They (**4.**) *can't / have to* create new laws to help reduce emissions.

HOST: Do we need new taxes to pay for this?

ACTIVIST: No, we (**5.**) *don't have to / must* have new taxes. There are other ways to raise money.

HOST: Any other thoughts?

ACTIVIST: Sometimes people feel that this problem is impossible to solve, but we (**6.**) *must not / don't have to* quit. And we (**7.**) *must / can't* have everyone's help.

HOST: We're out of time, so we (**8.**) *don't have to / have to* stop now. Thanks very much.

ACTIVIST: Thank you.

3 *Work with a partner. Read the list of suggestions and discuss which we **have to / must** do, **don't have to** do, and **must not** do to reduce our personal carbon footprints.*

1. build more public transportation
2. stop using electricity
3. ignore the problem of global warming
4. buy a carbon offset
5. stop using gasoline-powered cars
6. reduce factory emissions
7. drive big cars
8. ride bicycles

Example

STUDENT A: I think that we *must* build more public transportation.
STUDENT B: I agree. We *have to* stop driving everywhere. We *must not* rely on cars so much.

C SPEAKING

PRONUNCIATION: Intonation—Are you finished?

When you finish speaking, your voice should fall to a low note. When you have more to say but need some time to think, your voice doesn't fall to a low note.

CD 2
42 Listen to the way *I know* is pronounced in this conversation.

A: If you're worried about the environment, you shouldn't drive to work.
B: I know.
A: You should take the bus.
B: I know . . . but I think it's faster when I drive.

You can use *I know* to agree or disagree. When we use *I know* to disagree, we often follow it with *but*.

1 CD 2
43 *Listen to the sentences. Is the speaker finished or not? If the speaker is finished, put a period (.) after the sentence. If the speaker is going to continue, put an ellipsis (. . .). Check your answers with a partner's.*

1. I'm going to start riding my bike to work

2. I'm not going to use the air conditioner so much

3. I'm going to volunteer to clean up the park

4. I always turn the lights off when I go out

5. I drive to school once a week

6. I'm going to buy a hybrid[1]

7. I'm going to vote for green candidates

8. I'm going to recycle bottles and cans

2 *Look at the unfinished sentences in Exercise 1. Choose a sentence and finish it. Say your sentence to the class.*

3 *Work with a partner. Practice using your voice to let your partner know whether you've finished speaking or not. Read the sentences in Exercise 1 to your partner. Let your voice fall if your sentence is finished. Don't let your voice fall if your sentence isn't finished. Your partner will tell you whether he or she thinks your sentence is finished or not. Then switch roles.*

4 *Work with a partner. You will read statements about the environment to your partner. Your partner will give his or her opinion using* **I know and I because . . .** *or* **I know, but . . .** *Student A, your statements are on this page. Student B, your statements are on page 190.*

Student A's Statements

1. I don't think there's anything we can do about CO_2 levels. We all produce carbon dioxide when we breathe.

2. Wealthy countries create more pollution than poorer countries. They should have to pay to clean it up.

3. I'm worried about global warming, but I don't know if I can do anything to make a difference.

---

[1]**hybrid:** A car that uses electric power at lower speeds and gasoline power at higher speeds. It produces less pollution.

◀ FUNCTION: Taking Turns and Holding the Floor

1 *Look at the cartoon and answer the questions.*

1. Where are the man and the woman?

2. What is the man doing?

3. How is the woman responding to him?

Interrupting Politely

During a group discussion you can politely interrupt other speakers and take a turn. A person might interrupt to share an idea or opinion, to ask a question, or to ask someone to repeat.

STRATEGIES FOR INTERRUPTING POLITELY			
Sounds and Gestures	**Words to Ask for Clarification / Explanation**		**Words to Make a Comment**
Clear your throat (say "ahem").	I'm sorry, could you …? Could you … please? Excuse me, could you …?	… repeat that … explain that … say that again	I'd like to … … add something. … make a point.
Raise your hand. Raise your index finger. Make eye contact with the speaker.	Excuse me, can I …? I'm sorry, could I …?	… ask you a question … ask you something	But … Can I say something?

Holding the Floor

If you are speaking and someone interrupts, you can "hold the floor," or keep talking, if you aren't ready to be interrupted.

STRATEGIES FOR HOLDING THE FLOOR	
Sounds and Gestures	**Words for Holding the Floor**
Keep talking.	Just a minute / second.
Speak louder.	Hold on a minute / second.
Don't look at the person interrupting.	Let me finish, please.
Put your hand up to show that you want the other person to wait.	I'm not done yet.

NOTE: When interrupting and holding the floor, it is usually most effective to combine sounds and gestures with the words and phrases.

2 *Work with a partner to complete the classroom discussion. In the blanks write phrases for interrupting and holding the floor. Then practice the conversation in a group of three. Take turns with each role.*

KYOO HYUN: . . . So, what are the effects of global warming? One is that cyclones are bigger and more frequent. . . .

BRIDGET: (asking for clarification) (**1.**) _____, could you repeat that?

KYOO HYUN: Cyclones. They're getting bigger and more frequent.

BRIDGET: (asking for clarification) (**2.**) _____

KYOO HYUN: Yes?

BRIDGET: What's a cyclone?

KYOO HYUN: Oh, it's a really big storm that has very fast wind, like a hurricane. As I was saying . . .

SAM: (making a comment) (**3.**) _____ There have been a lot of strong cyclones recently, but I thought that it might not be caused by global warming.

(continued on next page)

KYOO HYUN: Some people say that, but most scientists don't agree.

SAM: (making a comment) (4.) _____ I've heard that . . .

KYOO HYUN: (holding the floor) (5.) _____. I want to finish this idea. . . .

3 *Work in a small group. Discuss the question for four minutes. Each person should interrupt at least once to share an idea or opinion, ask a question, or ask someone to repeat. Each person should also hold the floor at least once if he or she is interrupted. Use the strategies listed on pages 166 and 167.*

What can individuals, government, and industry do to reduce carbon emissions?

◖ **PRODUCTION:** Participating in a Seminar

In a seminar, there is usually a small group of students with a leader. The leader presents information to the group and leads a discussion. In this activity, **each student will take turns being the leader and the other students will participate in the discussion**. Try to use the vocabulary, grammar, pronunciation, and strategies for interrupting politely and holding the floor that you learned in the unit.*

Work in a group of four or five. Follow the steps.

Step 1: Choose a seminar topic. Each group member should choose a different topic.

Topic 1: global CO_2 emissions (Figures 1–2, page 169; discussion questions, page 190)

Topic 2: transportation (Figure 3, page 169; discussion questions, page 190)

Topic 3: CO_2 emissions and food production (Figure 4, page 170; discussion questions, page 191)

Topic 4: natural disasters and global warming (Figure 5, page 171; discussion questions, page 191)

Topic 5: sea level rise and global warming (Figure 6, page 172; discussion questions, page 191)

Step 2: Prepare for the seminar. You will become the expert on your topic.

- Study the information about your topic. Look at the figure and the discussion questions for your topic only. Make sure you understand all of the vocabulary.
- Think of an additional discussion question.
- You can also work with students from other groups who have the same topic.

---

*For Alternative Speaking Topics, see page 172.

Step 3: With your seminar group, take turns leading a discussion on your topic using the discussion questions. Make sure to refer to your figure during the discussion.

Topic 1: Global CO_2 Emissions

A country's carbon dioxide emissions can be measured in two ways: the *total amount* of CO_2 produced by the whole country (figure 1) or the amount of CO_2 produced by *each person* (figure 2).

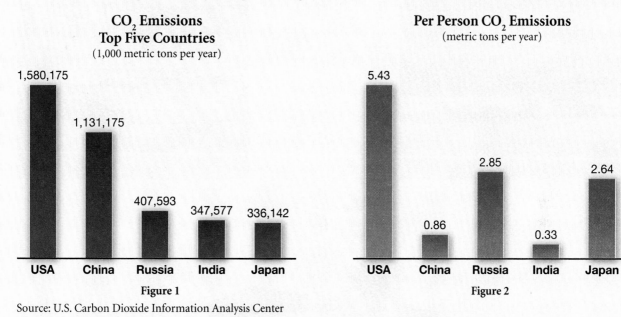

CO_2 Emissions
Top Five Countries
(1,000 metric tons per year)

USA 1,580,175
China 1,131,175
Russia 407,593
India 347,577
Japan 336,142

Figure 1

Per Person CO_2 Emissions
(metric tons per year)

USA 5.43
China 0.86
Russia 2.85
India 0.33
Japan 2.64

Figure 2

Source: U.S. Carbon Dioxide Information Analysis Center

Topic 2: Transportation

Transportation produces about 20 percent of CO_2 emissions. Cars and trucks are a major source of emissions. Figure 3 shows the percentage of cars and trucks in different parts of the world.

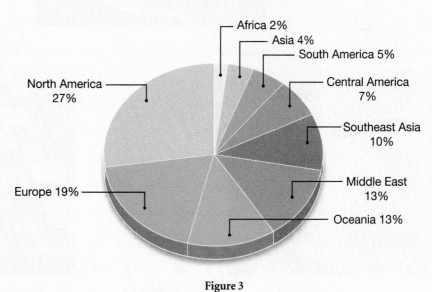

Cars and Trucks by Region

Africa 2%
Asia 4%
South America 5%
Central America 7%
Southeast Asia 10%
Middle East 13%
Oceania 13%
North America 27%
Europe 19%

Figure 3

Source: Nationmaster
http://www.nationmaster.com/graph/tra_mot_veh-transportation-motor-vehicles

Topic 3: CO_2 Emissions and Food Production

The process of growing, preparing, and selling food creates CO_2 emissions. Figure 4 shows examples of the emissions produced to make a box of breakfast cereal.

CO_2 Emissions from Producing Breakfast Cereal

1. Growing the food

2. Preparing and packaging the food

3. Transporting and selling the food in stores

4. Disposing of the packaging

Figure 4

Topic 4: Natural Disasters and Global Warming

Figure 5 shows the rise in weather-related disasters compared to earthquakes, which are not related to the weather.

Rise of Weather-Related Disasters Compared to Earthquakes

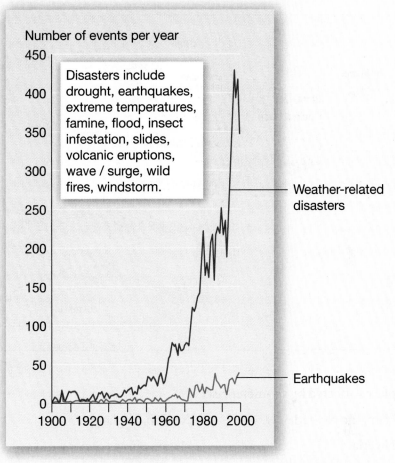

Figure 5

Source: "Trends in natural disasters." *UNEP/GRID-Arendal Maps and Graphics Library.* 2005. UNEP/GRID-Arendal. 28 Sep 2007 <http://maps.grida.no/go/graphic/trends-in-natural-disasters>. *Emmanuelle Bournay, Cartographer. UNEP/GRID-Arendal*

Topic 5: Sea Level Rise and Global Warming

Global warming may cause ice in the North and South Poles to melt. The melted ice will cause sea levels to rise. The red areas show places that will be underwater after six-meter (19.7-foot) sea level rise.

Areas at Risk from Sea Level Rise

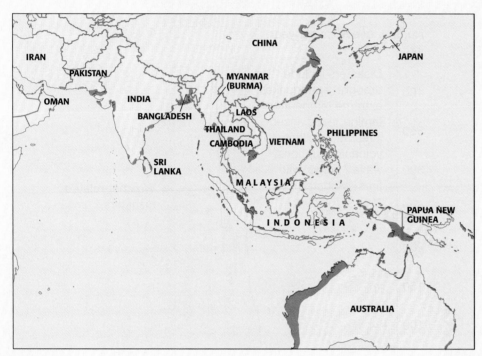

Source: Jeremy L. Weiss and Jonathan Overpeck. Environmental Studies Laboratory, Department of Geosciences, University of Arizona

Figure 6

Other places affected by six-meter rise:

Amsterdam, the Netherlands	London, England	New York, United States
Lagos, Nigeria	Miami, United States	Vancouver, Canada

ALTERNATIVE SPEAKING TOPICS

Discuss one of the topics. Use the vocabulary and grammar from the unit.

1. How has global warming affected you or your community? Have you seen any effects of global warming? What are people doing to reduce carbon emissions? Explain.

2. What lifestyle changes could you make to reduce your own carbon footprint?

RESEARCH TOPICS, see page 196.

To Spank or Not to Spank?

1 FOCUS ON THE TOPIC

A PREDICT

Discuss the questions with the class.

1. Look at the picture. Why do you think the parent is spanking the child? What did the child do? Do you think corporal punishment[1] is a good punishment in this case?

2. Read the title of the unit. What do you think this unit will be about?

---

[1]**corporal punishment:** punishment by hitting or spanking

173

SHARE INFORMATION

Discuss the questions in a small group. Then share your ideas with the class.

1. How did your parents punish you when you were a child? How did you feel about the punishment then? How do you feel about it now?

2. As a child, how did you learn right from wrong?

C **BACKGROUND** AND **VOCABULARY**

1 🔘 *Read and listen to the online parenting chat with a child psychologist.*

Parenting Chat with Dr. Beverly Lau, Child Psychologist

Dr. Lau: Welcome to the parenting chat!

Daddio: My son is six and my daughter is four. They love to play a fighting game, but sometimes my son (**1**) **gets carried away** and hurts his sister. He doesn't mean to hurt her. What can I do?

Dr. Lau: You need to (**2**) **set limits** for your son. Tell him he can't play the fighting game anymore. Suggest other games they can play.

Mommy1: What do you think about TV? I don't want my kids to watch TV, but my husband is very (**3**) **permissive**. He lets them watch whenever they want.

Dr. Lau: I always (**4**) **advocate** turning off the TV. But you and your husband need to do some (**5**) **problem solving** and agree on TV rules for your family.

Worried: Last week a neighbor was (**6**) **arrested** for child (**7**) **abuse**. He was hitting his children almost every day. Now my eight-year-old daughter has bad dreams every night. What can I do?

Dr. Lau: I understand why your daughter is upset. Talk to her about her feelings. Tell her she's safe. Hopefully, this is a (**8**) **short-term** problem and will go away in a few weeks. If not, talk to her doctor.

Newmom: My son is one year old. He thinks it's funny to hit me. How can I (**9**) **discipline** him when he does this?

Dr. Lau: Say "No hitting," and walk away. At his age, he's too young to understand the (**10**) **consequences** of his (**11**) **misbehavior**. He doesn't understand that he's hurting you.

Dad2teen: Yesterday, my son's high school teacher took his cell phone away and won't give it back. Is it legal for the teacher to keep it?

Dr. Lau: Talk to the principal. I think the teacher has a (**12**) **right** to take the phone away during school hours, but he should give it back at the end of school.

---

2 *Match the words and phrases on the left with the definitions on the right.*

_____ **1.** get carried away

_____ **2.** set limits

_____ **3.** permissive

_____ **4.** advocate

_____ **5.** problem solving

_____ **6.** arrested

_____ **7.** abuse

_____ **8.** short-term

_____ **9.** discipline

_____ **10.** consequences

_____ **11.** misbehavior

_____ **12.** right

a. cruel or violent treatment of someone

b. acting in a way that other people don't like

c. finding solutions

d. happening for a short period of time

e. make rules about what someone can and can't do

f. not strict; allowing activity that other people disapprove of

g. something you are allowed to do according to the law

h. strongly support

i. the results of an action

j. to be taken away by the police

k. to get so angry, excited, or interested that you are not in control of your actions

l. to punish someone

②FOCUS ON LISTENING

A LISTENING ONE: The Spanking Debate

🅒🅓2
45 *Listen to an excerpt from a radio report. Check (✓) your predictions.*

1. What opinion do you think will be presented in the report? Why?

_____ supporting spanking (thinking it's good)

_____ opposing spanking (thinking it's bad)

_____ both opinions

2. The reporter interviews several different people. Which people do you think will give their opinion about spanking? Why?

_____ police officer   _____ child

_____ doctor   _____ teacher

_____ parent   _____ lawyer

◖ LISTEN FOR MAIN IDEAS

🎵 CD 2 46 Listen to the report. Do the speakers support spanking or oppose spanking? Check (✓) each person's opinion. Write at least one reason for each opinion.

SPEAKER	SUPPORTS	OPPOSES	REASON(S)
1. Tyler Robinson			
2. Rhonda Moore			
3. Dr. Beverly Lau			
4. John Simmons			

◖ LISTEN FOR DETAILS

🎵 CD 2 47 Listen again to all the opinions and reasons the speakers give. What does each speaker believe about spanking? Write **Y** (yes) if the statement expresses the speaker's beliefs. Write **N** (no) if the statement does not express the speaker's beliefs.

Tyler Robinson

_____ **1.** Spanking teaches children to respect their parents.

_____ **2.** Spanking teaches children to solve problems with violence.

Rhonda Moore

_____ **3.** Pain helps children learn right and wrong.

_____ **4.** Spanking is done out of anger.

_____ **5.** Her children don't understand why they are spanked.

Dr. Beverly Lau

_____ **6.** Spanking teaches children to behave when their parents aren't around.

_____ **7.** If a child misbehaves there should be a consequence.

_____ **8.** Parents sometimes get carried away and hit too hard when they spank their children.

John Simmons

_____ **9.** Parents know their children best.

_____ **10.** The government should tell parents how to discipline their children.

◖ MAKE INFERENCES

Listen to the excerpts from the listening. How would each speaker respond to the statements? If the speaker would agree with the statement, write **agree** in the box. If the speaker would disagree, write **disagree**. If there isn't enough information to know, leave the box blank.

	EXCERPT 1 ROBINSON	EXCERPT 2 MOORE	EXCERPT 3 LAU
1. Parents should tell children what is right and what is wrong.			
2. Parents should listen to children's ideas.			
3. Children learn by watching their parents' behavior.			

◖ EXPRESS OPINIONS

Discuss the questions in a small group.

1. Which speaker do you think has the most convincing arguments? Why?

2. What are some effective ways to discipline a child? Why are they effective?

B LISTENING TWO: Parents' Rights vs. Children's Rights

CD 2
51 *Listen to a university lecture about corporal punishment. Fill in the missing notes.*

Parents' Rights versus Children's Rights

1. Rights of _____
- parents have a right to _____
- under the law _____
    exception: _____

2. Rights of _____
- human rights = _____
- under this view, spanking _____
- several countries have made spanking illegal
    first country: _____
- United Nations recommends: _____

_____

C INTEGRATE LISTENINGS ONE AND TWO

STEP 1: Organize

Work with a partner. Using the information from Listenings One and Two, make a list of arguments supporting and opposing spanking.

ARGUMENTS SUPPORTING SPANKING	ARGUMENTS OPPOSING SPANKING
• spanking helps set clear limits	• spanking teaches children to fear parents

Work with a different partner. Use the information from Step 1 to discuss the topic of spanking. Student A takes the pro position (supporting spanking). Student B takes the con position (opposing spanking). Then switch partners again and repeat the activity. This time argue the opposite position.

③ FOCUS ON SPEAKING

Ⓐ VOCABULARY

◀ REVIEW

Cross out the word or phrase below each sentence that has a different meaning from the boldfaced word or phrase. Use a dictionary to look up words you don't know.

1. Most psychologists don't **recommend** spanking children.

   a. advise   **b.** ~~like~~

2. Parents have **a right** to use spanking as a way to teach their children.

   a. permission   **b.** a need

3. I never **get carried away** and hit too hard when I spank my children.

   a. get arrested   **b.** lose control

4. Spanking is a **short-term** solution to bad behavior.

   a. temporary   **b.** possible

5. In some places, it is **illegal** for teachers to hit their students.

   a. all right   **b.** not permitted

6. The lawyer discussed the **issue** of corporal punishment.

   a. example   **b.** topic

7. I think spanking is a form of **abuse**.

   a. love   **b.** violence

8. Parents need to **set limits** for their children, so they can learn right from wrong.

   a. make rules   **b.** take classes with

9. Parents sometimes use spanking to punish a child's **misbehavior**.

   a. wrongdoing   **b.** intelligence

10. If a child does something wrong, there should be a **consequence** for his or her behavior.

    a. an effect   **b.** a reason

1 CD 2 ⟨52⟩ *Read and listen to the conversation about making spanking illegal.*

HOST: Should it be against the law to spank your children? Today we're talking about the **pros and cons** of corporal punishment. With us are Dr. Beverly Lau, a child psychologist, and John Simmons, a family law attorney. Dr. Lau, do you agree that we should have a law against spanking?

DR. LAU: I do. We have to **take a hard line** and say that hitting a child is wrong. Corporal punishment is bad for children.

MR. SIMMONS: I disagree. **The bottom line** is this: Do we want government controlling how we raise our children? That's the question you have to ask.

DR. LAU: No, this issue is **black and white**. Study after study shows that spanking isn't effective and can be harmful to kids. And there's **a fine line** between spanking and child abuse.

MR. SIMMONS: I agree that spanking is bad, but I **draw the line at** making spanking illegal. It's the wrong approach. And I think that, **by and large**, most people would agree with me!

HOST: Clearly, we need some more **give and take** to find a position that both sides can agree on. We'll be back after this break.

2 *Write the boldfaced expressions from the conversation in the correct spaces. Then match the meaning with the expressions by writing the letters in the blanks.*

Expressions with *line*

    c   take a hard line   **a.** a small difference

_____ _____   **b.** the most important point

_____ _____   **c̶.** be unwilling to change your opinion

_____ _____   **d.** say "no" to something

Expressions with *and*

_____ _____   **e.** share ideas and opinions

_____ _____   **f.** the good points and bad points

_____ _____   **g.** has one clearly correct position

_____ _____   **h.** generally speaking

◖ CREATE

Divide into two groups, A and B.
First, Group A students conduct Survey A. Ask three students all of the questions.
Group B students answer the questions and give reasons, using the words from the box in their answers.
Then Group B students conduct Survey B.

SURVEY A	ANSWERS		
	Student 1	Student 2	Student 3
1. Is it important for parents and children to have give and take when they discuss problems? Why or why not?			
2. When children misbehave, should they help to decide the consequences? Why or why not?			
3. Is there a fine line between discipline and child abuse? Why or why not?			

SURVEY B	ANSWERS		
	Student 1	Student 2	Student 3
1. Do you think that, by and large, most parents support or oppose spanking? Why or why not?			
2. Does the government have the right to control how parents raise their children? Why or why not?			
3. Should countries take a hard line and make spanking illegal? Why or why not?			

acceptable	debate	legal	punish
arrest	draw the line	limits	respect
black-and-white issue	get carried away	permissive	short-term
the bottom line	the law	problem solving	violent

1 *Read the excerpt from a magazine article. Notice the boldfaced verbs. Then answer the questions.*

> The number of parents in the United States who spank their children **has decreased** in the past 50 years. Public opinion about spanking **has changed**. Many doctors **have warned** that spanking is harmful—or is even a form of child abuse, and in response, parents **have learned** new ways to discipline their children. Over the past 10 years, more and more parents **have switched** to problem solving and logical consequences as their primary methods of discipline.

1. When did public opinion about spanking change?

2. When did parents switch to problem solving as a primary method of discipline?

PRESENT PERFECT TENSE	
1. Use the present perfect ...	
• to talk about things that happened at an *indefinite time* in the past.	Many doctors **have warned** that spanking is harmful. (We don't know when they said this.)
• to talk about things that *started in the past, continue in the present, and may continue into the future.*	During the past 10 years, most parents **have switched** from spanking to problem solving as their main method of discipline. (Ten years ago parents started to discipline differently, and they will probably continue to do this.)
2. Use *has / have just* to talk about events that happened not too long ago in the past.	Some countries **have just decided** to make spanking against the law. (It's a new law that was passed recently.)
3. To form the present perfect, use *have / has (not)* **+ the past participle**.	The problems of parenting **have (not) changed**.
To form *yes / no questions*, begin with *have / has*.	**Have** you **talked** with your doctor about parenting issues?
To form *wh- questions*, begin with a *wh-* word.	**Why have** you **stopped** spanking your child?

2 Read the interview with a psychologist about child discipline. Complete the questions (Q) and answers (A) with the present perfect.

Q: How **(1.)** _____have_____ parents' beliefs about spanking

_____changed_____ in the past 50 years in the United States?
   (change)

A: Many parents **(2.)** _____ using spanking as their first method of
                         (stop)

discipline.

Q: What type of discipline **(3.)** _____ parents _____
                                                                      (use)

instead?

A: I think parents **(4.)** _____ talking to the children more.
                         (start)

Q: But the number of crimes committed by children and teenagers

(5.) _____ in the past few years. Some people believe that this is
         (rise)

because parents **(6.)** _____ their children the difference between
                        (not / teach)

right and wrong.

A: Most doctors disagree. Research **(7.)** _____ that spanking
                                               (show)

actually makes kids more violent. That's why, for the past several years, doctors

(8.) _____ that parents use nonviolent methods of discipline.
         (recommend)

Q: The government **(9.)** _____ just _____ stronger
                                                       (pass)

laws against child abuse. Do you think that's a good idea?

A: Well, this year police **(10.)** _____ several parents for spanking
                                        (arrest)

their children. But I think parent education is more effective.

3 Work in a small group. Discuss the questions using the present perfect.

Over the past 50 years . . .

1. How have parents' methods of disciplining their children changed?
2. How have laws about punishing children changed?

◀ PRONUNCIATION: Final s and z

Sometimes it is difficult to say and hear the difference between the sound /z/ and the sound /s/ at the end of words.

Feel the difference between /z/ and /s/. Put two or three fingers along the side of your throat. Say "zzzzzzzz." What do you feel? Then say "ssssssss." What do you feel? Then say "zzzzzssssssszzzzzzzssssssss." What happens when you change between /z/ and /s/?

FINAL S AND Z			
/z/ is a *voiced* consonant. The vocal chords vibrate ("buzz") when you say this sound.	raise	prize	faze
/s/ is a *voiceless* consonant. The vocal chords don't vibrate.	race	price	face
NOTE: Some nouns and verbs are spelled the same, but are pronounced differently. • The verbs end in the /z/ sound. • The nouns end in the /s/ sound.	/z/ to abuse to excuse to use /s/ child abuse a bad excuse a good use		

1 CD 2 53 *Listen to the final sounds in the underlined words. Put a check (✓) next to the sound you hear.*

1. He asked the counselor to <u>advise</u> him.　　 ＿＿ /s/　　 ＿＿ /z/

2. The counselor gave him some <u>advice</u>.　　 ＿＿ /s/　　 ＿＿ /z/

3. She has no <u>use</u> for spanking.　　 ＿＿ /s/　　 ＿＿ /z/

4. She doesn't <u>use</u> spanking to discipline her kids.　　 ＿＿ /s/　　 ＿＿ /z/

2 Listen to the words and repeat them.

/z/	/s/
abuse (verb)	abuse (noun)
lose	loose
peas	piece / peace
eyes	ice
fears	fierce
rise	rice
plays	place
knees	niece
advise	advice
raise	race

3 CD 2 Listen again. You will hear one word from each pair in Exercise 2. Circle the word you hear. Check your answers with the class.

4 Work with a partner. Take turns saying a word from each of the pairs in the list above to your partner. Your partner will repeat the word and point to either /z/ or /s/.

5 CD 2 Listen to the tongue twisters and repeat.

1. The advisor gave them some advice to raise race horses.

2. Did the police abuse Dale Clover's rights when they arrested him for child abuse?

3. My niece hurt her knees, so I placed some frozen peas on them.

4. My son fears that our neighbor's fierce dog will lose his collar and get loose.

Choose one of the tongue twisters, practice it, and say it to the class.

6 Work with a partner. Student A reads either sentence **a** or sentence **b** from item 1 in the left column. Student B listens and chooses the correct response, either sentence **c** or sentence **d**. Continue through the list. Then switch roles and repeat.

Sentence	**Response**
1. **a.** Did you get a good price?	**c.** Yes, it was very cheap.
b. Did you get a good prize?	**d.** Yes, I came in first.
2. **a.** Do you want peas?	**c.** No, I don't like them.
b. Do you want peace?	**d.** Yes, for the whole world.

3. **a.** I have blue ice.   **c.** How did you make it blue?

   b. I have blue eyes.   **d.** Does your mother have them, too?

4. **a.** I asked him for a raise.   **c.** Did you get the money?

   b. I asked him for a race.   **d.** Who won?

◖ FUNCTION: Expressing Confidence

Opinions can be expressed with different levels of confidence. When you sound more confident, your arguments are stronger.

1 *Read the opinions about spanking. Which opinion is expressed with more confidence? Which is expressed with less confidence?*

Opinion 1: Clearly, parents need to discipline their children. But we know for a fact that spanking is not effective.

Opinion 2: Generally, parents need to discipline their children. But in most cases, spanking is not effective.

EXPRESSING CONFIDENCE	LESS CONFIDENCE
More confidence Clearly, . . . It's clear that . . . There's no doubt . . . We know for a fact that . . . Obviously, . . .	**Less confidence** Generally, / Generally speaking, . . . In most cases, . . . It seems as if . . . You could say that . . .

2 *With a partner, take turns reading the statements aloud. Decide if the statement expresses more or less confidence. Then change the statement to have the other meaning.*

Example

It seems as if most parents spank their children occasionally. ___less confidence___

___It's clear that most parents spank their children occasionally.___

1. Clearly, young people today are more disrespectful to adults. _____

   _____

2. Usually, children will listen if they see that you are serious about discipline.

   _____

3. You could say that parents today are too permissive. _____

   _____

4. Obviously, you should spank your children if you want them to respect you.

   _____

5. In most cases, there needs to be stricter punishments at home. _____

   _____

6. It seems as if people are arguing against spanking these days. _____

   _____

7. We know for a fact that spanking is a short-term solution to behavior problems.

   _____

8. Generally, parents today have trouble disciplining their children. _____

   _____

9. You could say that there is a fine line between spanking and child abuse.

   _____

10. There's no doubt that people are unsure about how to raise their children.

   _____

◀ **PRODUCTION: Debate**

> In this activity, you will **debate a topic related to punishment**. In a debate, two teams discuss different sides of the same topic. One team is pro (for) a position on the topic. The other team is con (against) the position. Try to use the vocabulary, grammar, pronunciation, and language for expressing confidence that you learned in the unit.*

Work in two teams. Follow the steps. (If you have a large class, you may divide into groups and have several debates on different topics.)

Step 1: Read the topics and the background information that follows each topic. Choose one topic to debate. Decide which team will be pro and which will be con.

1. Teenagers should be punished as adults.

   In the United States, children and teenagers under age 18 who commit crimes are punished differently from adult criminals. They go to special jails, have shorter jail sentences, and cannot get the death penalty. In some states, courts are punishing children and teenagers like adults.

---

*For Alternative Speaking Topics, see page 189.

2. **Teachers should be able to use spanking to discipline their students.**

   In some countries, teachers can hit or spank their students when the students misbehave. In other countries, it is against the law for teachers to hit their students.

3. **Governments should use corporal punishment to punish criminals.**

   In some countries, the government uses corporal punishment (hitting or beating) to punish criminals. In other countries, the government can't use corporal punishment.

4. **Parents should be punished when their children do something wrong.**

   In the United States, some people want to pass a new law that says if a child under 18 does something wrong (such as stealing from a store or missing school), the parents will be punished because they did not control their child.

Step 2: Work with your team to prepare for the debate:

- Plan your arguments (points to support your position). Write an outline.

Example

> **Your team's position: Parents SHOULD NOT be allowed to spank their children.**
>
> **Argument 1:** Spanking isn't effective.
>
> **Explanation:** – It only stops behavior in the short term.
>
> – It doesn't teach kids to solve their problems.

- Think about the arguments the other team may make. Plan your counter-arguments (points you can use against the other team's arguments). Write an outline.

Example

> **Other team's position: Parents SHOULD be allowed to spank their children.**
>
> **Possible argument:** Spanking has been used for thousands of years as a type of discipline.
>
> **Counterargument:** Today we understand more about psychology and how spanking affects children.

Step 3: Debate the topic. The two teams take turns presenting their arguments and counterarguments. Team members should take turns presenting the information.

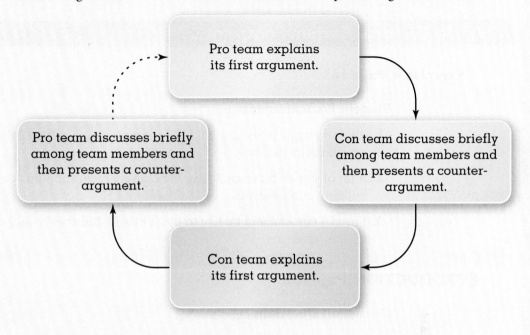

Repeat the process until both teams have presented all their arguments.

ALTERNATIVE SPEAKING TOPICS

Read the quotes about punishment. Do you agree with them? Why or why not? Share your thoughts with the class.

1. Quote: "Spare the rod and spoil the child."
   —Samuel Butler, poet

   Paraphrase: If you don't spank your children, they will be spoiled.

2. Quote: "The test of the morality of a society is what it does for its children."
   —Dietrich Bonhoffer, German pastor, Nazi resister

   Paraphrase: A good society treats its children well.

3. Quote: "My mother had a great deal of trouble with me, but I think she enjoyed it."
   —Mark Twain, author

   Paraphrase: I caused my mother a lot of trouble, but I think she enjoyed raising me.

RESEARCH TOPICS, see page 196.

STUDENT ACTIVITIES

UNIT 9: Personal Carbon Footprint

Exercise 4, Page 165

Student B's Statements

1. A lot of people in the automobile industry are going to lose their jobs if we raise taxes on gasoline.

2. A lot of storms hit coastal areas. The government shouldn't permit new building in coastal areas.

3. I need a new car, and I'd like to buy a hybrid. But they're more expensive than gas-powered cars.

◀ PRODUCTION, Page 168

Discussion Questions

Topic 1: Global CO_2 Emissions

1. Look at Figure 1. Which countries produce the most and least total CO_2 emissions?

2. Look at Figure 2. Which countries produce the most and least CO_2 emissions per person?

3. Why do you think some countries have high total emissions but low per person emissions?

4. Do you think these countries can all lower their CO_2 emissions in the same way? How should their approaches be similar or different?

5. Your question: _____

Topic 2: Transportation

1. Look at Figure 3. Which areas of the world have the most cars? Which have the least?

2. Why do you think there is such a big difference in the number of cars and trucks in different parts of the world? Do you think that will change in the future, or stay the same?

3. How can we convince people to stop buying and driving cars?

4. Your question: _____

Topic 3: CO_2 Emissions and Food Production

1. Look at Figure 4. For each step in producing the breakfast cereal, how are CO_2 emissions made?

2. Think about these foods: tomatoes grown in your backyard, hamburger meat (beef), chocolate. Do you think that preparing these foods emits more or less CO_2 than preparing the breakfast cereal? Explain your answer.

3. What foods can we eat to help lower CO_2 emissions?

4. Your question: _____

Topic 4: Natural Disasters and Global Warming

1. Look at Figure 5. What types of disasters have increased since 1900? What types of disasters have stayed about the same?

2. Why do you think weather disasters have increased, but earthquakes have not?

3. What are some effects of weather disasters?

4. Your question: _____

Topic 5: Sea Level Rise and Global Warming

1. Look at Figure 6. What do the red areas show?

2. What places will be most affected by sea level rise?

3. What will happen to the people who live in the areas close to a sea?

4. Think about where you live. What areas do you think might be affected by sea level rise?

5. Your question: _____

RESEARCH TOPICS

UNIT 1: Advertising on the Air

◖ RESEARCH

Step 1: Find three magazine ads that grab your attention and bring them to class.

Step 2: Work in small groups. Show your ads to the group and discuss the questions.

1. Who is the target audience?

2. What techniques does the advertiser use to sell the product?

3. Do you think this ad is effective? Why or why not?

UNIT 2: Identity Theft

◖ RESEARCH

Step 1: Find out more about identity theft. Choose one topic from the box or think of your own.

child identity theft	dumpster diving	shoulder surfing
criminal identity theft	mortgage fraud	skimming
data theft	phishing	

Step 2: Research the topic on the Internet or in the library. Use the questions to guide your research.

1. What is _____?

2. Is it a common way to commit identity theft?

3. What can people do to protect themselves against _____?

4. What are some other interesting facts about _____?

Step 3: Share your information with the class.

UNIT 3: Endurance Test

◖ RESEARCH

Step 1: Choose an extreme sport from the box or think of your own.

bungee jumping	extreme skiing	ironman triathlon
cave diving	free-diving	kite boarding
class 5 river rafting	hang gliding	parasailing
cliff diving	ice climbing	rappelling
deep sea diving	Iditarod	sky diving

Step 2: Research the sport on the Internet or in the library. Find a picture of the sport and answer the questions.

1. What do you do in this sport?

2. What is dangerous about this sport?

3. Why do people like this sport?

4. What other information can you find about this sport?

Step 3: Present your picture and information to the class.

UNIT 4: Separated by the Same Language

◖ RESEARCH

Step 1: Choose a group of people who have their own slang (teenagers, musicians, college students) or jargon[1] (computer programmers, medical professionals).

Step 2: Interview a person from that group and take notes. Ask the person to tell you about special slang or jargon the group uses. Then ask him or her to explain the meaning of five words or phrases. You can also find dictionaries of slang words on the Internet (keywords = *slang* and *jargon*) or in the library to add to your research.

Step 3: Report to the class. Tell them what group of people you researched. Then write the slang or jargon on the board (but not the definitions). See if your classmates can guess the meaning of the words.

---

[1]**jargon:** technical words or phrases usually associated with a profession or field (e.g., computer jargon)

UNIT 5: Culture and Commerce

◀ RESEARCH

Some tourists use their vacation time to help others or help the environment. For example, a volunteer could go to Tanzania and build homes for poor people. These types of vacations are called "service vacations" or "volunteer vacations."

Step 1: Do research to find an example of a service vacation. You can . . .

- look for service vacations or volunteer vacations on the Internet.
- look for brochures or magazines about service vacations from environmental groups (for example, EarthWatch) or human aid groups (for example, Global Volunteers).

Step 2: Prepare a short report to share with the class. Use the questions to guide your research.

1. What is the destination of this vacation?

2. What can you do on this vacation?

3. Can people who choose this vacation really help the environment or the people who live nearby? If so, how? If not, why not?

4. Would you go on this vacation? Why or why not?

Step 3: Present your report to the class.

UNIT 6: The Art of Storytelling

◀ RESEARCH

Step 1: Find a recorded story at the library or on the Internet, or ask a friend or relative to tell you a story. Listen to the story. (If you can't find a story in English, listen to one in your native language.)

Step 2: Prepare a summary of the story using the questions.

1. What is the name of the story?

2. Who told the story?

3. Who are the main characters? Give a one-sentence description of each character.

4. What happens in the story? Give a brief summary of the plot.

5. Do you like this story? Why or why not?

Step 3: Present your summary to the class, or make a recording of your summary and give it to your teacher.

UNIT 7: Voluntary Simplicity

◖ RESEARCH

Simple living is an idea that has become popular in many western countries. Many people are tired of their fast-paced way of life and want to make a change.

Step 1: Choose one of the topics from the box or think of your own.

affluenza	organic farming	take back your time
clutter free	simplicity circle	un-jobbing
co-housing	slow food	voluntary simplicity
freegan		

Step 2: Research the topic on the Internet or in the library. Use the questions to guide your research.

1. What is _____?

2. Why are people interested in _____?

3. How does _____ fit in with the goals of the simple living lifestyle?

Step 3: Present your findings to the class.

UNIT 8: Before You Say "I Do"

◖ RESEARCH

Step 1: In this activity, you will research an alternative marriage practice. Choose one of the topics from the box or think of your own.

civil unions	mail-order / Internet brides	polygamy
dowry	matchmakers	serial monogamy

Step 2: Research the topic on the Internet or in the library. Use the questions to guide your research.

1. What is / are _____?

2. In what cultures might you find _____?

3. Would _____ be legal in your culture? Why or why not?

4. What do you think about _____? Why do you feel this way?

Step 3: Meet in small groups with students who chose different marriage practices. Present the results of your research and have a discussion.

UNIT 9: Personal Carbon Footprint

◖ RESEARCH

There are many services and technologies that can help lower carbon emissions, including:

- Transportation: car sharing services (for example, Zip Car, I-GO), hybrid electric cars, biofuel, bicycle sharing programs
- Electrical use: Energy Star appliances, compact fluorescent light bulbs, wind power, solar power, hydropower
- Heating and cooling: green buildings, solar heat, eco-roofs, insulation, geothermal
- Business and industry: tree planting programs, CO_2 emissions trading, green product design

Step 1: Do research on the Internet about a service or technology that reduces carbon emissions. Find out how it works, how much it costs, and how it reduces carbon emissions.

Step 2: Share your research in a small group or with the class.

UNIT 10: To Spank or Not to Spank?

◖ RESEARCH

Step 1: Visit a place where you can see adults taking care of young children. For example, a nursery school or preschool, a playground, or a friend or relative who has children. Watch the children and adults for an hour or so. Look for times when a child misbehaves and an adult disciplines the child. Use the chart to take notes about what you see.

WHY DID THE ADULTS DISCIPLINE THE CHILD(REN)?	HOW DID THE ADULTS DISCIPLINE THE CHILD(REN)?	WAS IT EFFECTIVE?
A child threw something at another child.	An adult yelled and told the child not to throw things.	No. Child continued throwing after the adult left.

Here are some things an adult may do to discipline a child (also look for other things that are not on this list):

- Say "No" to the child
- Take something away from the child
- Move the child to a different place
- Make the child sit by himself or herself
- Hold the child so he or she can't do something
- Yell at the child in a loud voice
- Hit or spank the child

Step 2: Write a report on what you observed. Use the questions to guide you.

1. What types of discipline did you see? Was the discipline violent or nonviolent?

2. Did the discipline make the child stop misbehaving? Why or why not?

3. What does this type of discipline teach a child?

4. How was the discipline the same or different from other types of discipline you have seen or experienced?

Step 3: Share your research in a small group or with the class.

GRAMMAR BOOK REFERENCES

NorthStar: Listening and Speaking Level 3, Third Edition	Focus on Grammar Level 3, Third Edition	Azar's Fundamentals of English Grammar, Third Edition
Unit 1 Simple Present and Present Progressive	**Unit 1** Present Progressive and Simple Present	**Chapter 1** Present Time
Unit 2 Modals of Advice	**Unit 14** Advice: *Should, Ought to, Had better*	**Chapter 7** Modal Auxiliaries: 7-7, 7-8
Unit 3 Reflexive and Reciprocal Pronouns	**Unit 9** Reflexive and Reciprocal Pronouns	**Chapter 6** Nouns and Pronouns: 6-13
Unit 4 Modals of Ability and Possibility	**Unit 11** Ability: *Can, Could, Be able to* **Unit 36** Future Possibility: *May, Might, Could*	**Chapter 7** Modal Auxiliaries: 7-2, 7-3
Unit 5 Future Predictions with *If-Clauses*	**Unit 6** Future	**Chapter 3** Future Time: 3-6

NorthStar: Listening and Speaking Level 3, Third Edition	Focus on Grammar Level 3, Third Edition	Azar's Fundamentals of English Grammar, Third Edition
Unit 6 Infinitives of Purpose	**Unit 30** Infinitives of Purpose	**Chapter 13** Gerunds and Infinitives: 13-9
Unit 7 Nouns and Quantifiers	**Unit 21** Nouns and Quantifiers	**Chapter 11** Count/Noncount Nouns and Articles: 11-2–11-7
Unit 8 Comparatives and Equatives	**Unit 24** Adjectives: Comparisons with As … as and Than	**Chapter 9** Comparisons
Unit 9 Modals of Necessity	**Unit 34** Necessity: Have (got) to, Must, Don't have to, Must not, Can't	**Chapter 7** Modal Auxiliaries: 7-9, 7-10
Unit 10 Present Perfect Tense	**Unit 18** Present Perfect: Indefinite Past	**Chapter 4** The Present Perfect and the Past Perfect: 4-2–4-4

AUDIOSCRIPT

UNIT I: Advertising on the Air

2A. LISTENING ONE: *Advertising on the Air*

Professor: OK, let's get started now . . . Alright, now, as you remember, last week we talked about some basic appeals used in advertising . . . We talked a bit about informational appeals, that is, giving the consumer information about a product, like the price, or how it works, and so on. But today we're gonna talk about another type of appeal: an emotional appeal—an appeal to our feelings. This can be a positive appeal, emphasizing positive emotions like happiness or love, or a negative appeal, emphasizing negative emotions like fear or embarrassment.

LISTEN FOR MAIN IDEAS

Professor: OK, let's get started now . . . Alright, now, as you remember, last week we talked about some basic appeals used in advertising . . . We talked a bit about informational appeals, that is, giving the consumer information about a product, like the price, or how it works, and so on. But today we're gonna talk about another type of appeal: an emotional appeal—an appeal to our feelings. This can be a positive appeal, emphasizing positive emotions like happiness or love, or a negative appeal, emphasizing negative emotions like fear or embarrassment. Emotional appeals are very common, a very effective technique in advertising. Why are they so effective? Well, it's because no matter how much information you give a customer about a product, it's often their feelings about it that make the sale, not the information.

So today, I've brought in some radio ads to listen to, so you can see what I'm talking about. So, now we'll start with one of the most common emotional appeals, an appeal using humor.

Man: Hey, boy. [whistles] Come here!

Dog: [whines]

Man: Hey, what's the matter?

Dog: What's the matter? It's the dog food he's feeding me. It's terrible! Woof! But Spot, in the next yard . . . . he gets Doggie Delight dog food. Just look at it . . . delicious chunks of meat, tasty vegetables, all covered in creamy gravy! Please, please, I want Doggie Delight—woooo!

Announcer: Treat your dog right—get Doggie Delight!

Professor: OK, now, the humor here is the talking dog and the sound effects and so on. Now, you'll notice that the ad doesn't really give much information—just a bit about what's in the food—so it mostly relies on humor to sell the product.

Now, let's look specifically at some of the reasons humor is so effective in advertising. One reason is what you might call the "feel-good" factor. That is, humor just makes us feel good, makes us laugh, and that gives us a positive feeling about the product. And that's what advertisers want—that positive feeling.

Another important reason is that, well, if an ad's funny, it gets our attention. Right? And really, with the huge number of ads we see and hear each day, that's the advertiser's number one problem: getting our attention. And a great thing about humor is it's very effective at getting our attention.

OK. Now let's listen to another ad, and pay attention to how humor is used in this one:

Voice: Thank you for calling Global Bank, the biggest bank in town. To assist you with your call, please enter your telephone number . . .

Voice: Please enter your zip code . . .

Voice: Please enter your birth date . . .

Voice: Please enter your shoe size . . . Please enter your lucky number . . .

Announcer: Does your bank think of you as just a number? At Neighbors' Bank, there's always someone here to answer your calls. Neighbors' Bank. Fast, convenient service with a personal touch.

Professor: OK, a bank is a serious product, right? So we could have an ad with a serious appeal, saying, "Neighbors' Bank has great service, we're the best" . . . and all that. But this ad uses humor. Why? Well, because it really gets your attention; it's a lot more interesting. So the consumer is more likely to listen to the ad and to remember it later. OK, any questions before we move on to another example? No? Alright, I'm gonna play some ads with a negative emotional appeal . . .

LISTEN FOR DETAILS

(Repeat Listen for Main Ideas)

MAKE INFERENCES

Ad 1: Doggie Delight

Man: Hey, boy. [whistles] Come here!

Dog: [whines]

Man: Hey, what's the matter?

Dog: What's the matter? It's the dog food he's feeding me. It's terrible! Woof! But Spot, in the next yard . . . he gets Doggie Delight dog food. Just look at it . . . delicious chunks of meat, tasty vegetables, all covered in creamy gravy! Please, please, I want Doggie Delight—woooo!

Announcer: Treat your dog right—get Doggie Delight!

Ad 2: Neighbors' Bank

Voice: Thank you for calling Global Bank, the biggest bank in town. To assist you with your call, please enter your telephone number . . .

Voice: Please enter your zip code . . .

Voice: Please enter your birth date . . .

Voice: Please enter your shoe size . . . Please enter your lucky number . . .

Announcer: Does your bank think of you as just a number? At Neighbors' Bank, there's always someone here to answer your calls. Neighbors' Bank. Fast, convenient service with a personal touch.

2B. LISTENING TWO: *Negative Appeals*

Thief Buster Ad

Announcer: You park your car, and your worst nightmare happens! When you come back . . . it's gone! It can happen anywhere . . . and chances are, one day, it will happen to you! That's why you need the incredible Thief Buster security system. Thief Buster calls the police, turns off your car engine, and the thief will get nowhere fast. Affordable and easy to install: get a Thief Buster security system today! Thief Buster . . . protection for your peace of mind!

Sunny Resorts Ad

Reporter: I'm standing here in Martin's office, and, as you can see, conditions are just terrible. The phone is ringing off the hook . . . his computer isn't working . . . and . . . wait . . . it looks like his boss is coming down the hall!

Boss: Martin!

Reporter: Martin, you gotta get outta here! Conditions are much better since Martin arrived for vacation here at Sunny Resorts. Right now he's lying on the beach, listening to the waves . . . sipping a cold drink . . . and enjoying life.

Announcer: Sunny Resorts. You deserve a vacation.

White Bright Ad

Child: The Color Yellow
            Yellow as the sun.
            Yellow as a ripe banana.
            Yellow as a sunflower.
            Yellow as my mommy's beautiful smile.

Announcer: Maybe your teeth aren't as white as you think. For a whiter, brighter smile, use White Bright. Just ten minutes a day. White Bright.

UNIT 2: Identity Theft

2A. LISTENING ONE: *Lily's Story*

Lily: So, by the end of the week, I was feeling totally helpless. And, like, a total victim. What do I do now? I have $30,000 worth of credit card bills in my name, with my address, and I felt really exposed. Somebody knows who I am, where I live, what my phone number is, and I'm helpless to stop this.

LISTEN FOR MAIN IDEAS

Announcer: Lily's wallet was stolen at a restaurant. The thief used her personal information to open credit cards in her name. But she had no idea she was the victim of identity theft. Then one day, she was home working on her computer when she got a call from a department store. In this story, Lily describes what happened next.

Lily: So, I was at the computer and the phone rang, I got this phone call, and she said, "Well, we have here that you've bought a diamond ring, so I'm just confirming the purchase because it's quite a bit of money." And I said, "Well, what is it?" And she said, "It's a $5,000 diamond ring." And I said, "No, I haven't left the house today, so I wouldn't have bought a diamond ring, and anyway, I don't go to that store, I don't go to your store anymore." And so, she said, "Well, somebody who has your name has purchased a diamond ring for $5,000." And I said, "$5,000! A diamond ring! Well, that's not me. I didn't buy it, and I don't authorize the purchase of this diamond ring, OK? So, we have a problem."

And she said, "We don't have a problem, I think, I hate to tell you this, you have a problem." And I said, "What are you talking about?" She said, "I hate to break the news to you, but I think that you have been a victim of identity theft." And I said, "A victim of what?" and she said, "Identity theft." And she said, "Well, when you get this bill . . ." And I said, "Excuse me? I'm going to get a bill for this?" She says, "Oh, Yes. When you get the bill, you need to file a complaint." And I said, "Oh, boy."

So, I did that, I filed the complaint. And then, it just went from bad to worse.

On Monday, I got home from work and I checked my mail and there was a bill from another department store, and another department store. On Tuesday, there were two more bills from two other department stores. On Wednesday, there were three bills from three consumer electronics stores. On Thursday, there were four bills from a jewelry store, a clothing store, another department store. By Friday, I had accumulated close to 38 or 39 bills. And I was up to probably close to $30,000 worth of charges, if not more. So, by the end of the week, I was feeling totally helpless. And, like, a total victim. What do I do now? I have thirty thousand dollars worth of credit card bills in my name, with my address, and I felt really exposed. Somebody knows who I am, where I live, what my phone number is, and I'm helpless to stop this.

So, what did I do? Every night, I had to deal with these bills. And what you have to do, is you have to make copies of the police report, etcetera, that, you know, my wallet was stolen. You have to describe in detail what they had purchased, and you have to write a letter to every single one of these stores that charged me, explaining what had happened. And you hope that they will not keep the charges there for you.

It took about, I would say, close to four months before the whole thing died away, and just a lot of time and a lot of worry. I worried a lot.

And the paranoia hasn't left, I mean, I'm still really conscious and nervous about receipts I have, I always rip them up into many tiny little pieces. And, the other thing that is really scary is how easy it is to open up credit cards. Shocking! You can go into any store, and you can just give them your name, your address, you don't need any proof of identification, and you can open up a credit card at that particular store. They don't really check who you are. How many clerks really look at the back of your credit card and check your signature? Not many.

There's all sorts of ways that your identity can be stolen. So, I think everybody should be paranoid.

LISTEN FOR DETAILS

(Repeat Listen for Main Ideas)

MAKE INFERENCES

Excerpt One

And so, she said, "Well, somebody who has your name has purchased a diamond ring for $5,000." And I said, "$5,000! A diamond ring! Well, that's not me. I didn't buy it, and I don't authorize the purchase of this diamond ring, OK? So, we have a problem."

Excerpt Two

And she said, "We don't have a problem, I think, I hate to tell you this, you have a problem." And I said, "What are you talking about?" She said, "I hate to break the news to you, but I think that you have been a victim of identity theft." And I said, "A victim of what?" and she said, "Identity theft."

Excerpt Three

And she said, "Well, when you get this bill . . ." And I said, "Excuse me? I'm going to get a bill for this?" She says, "Oh, Yes. When you get the bill, you need to file a complaint." And I said, "Oh, boy."

2B. LISTENING TWO: *Public Service Announcements*

Public Service Announcement 1

Company: American Bank VISA. May I help you?

Victim: Yes, I'm calling about my credit card bill. There's a charge for $4,000 that I KNOW I didn't make . . .

Announcer: Think you're safe from identity theft? Think again. Every minute, 19 people in the United States have their identities stolen. However, there *are* things that you can do to reduce your risk. First: Get a locked mailbox. Don't let a thief steal your mail and use it to steal your identity. Second: Be careful when someone asks you for personal information. Don't give out information over the phone, by mail, or on the Internet unless you *know* who you're dealing with. To see more tips on avoiding identity theft, visit the Identity Theft Helpline . . .

Public Service Announcement 2

Announcer: Hear that sound? That's the sound of a crime being committed. Everyday, criminals find personal information from papers that we throw away. It doesn't take much—a name, an address, an ID number—and the thief has all he needs to commit identity theft.

Hear that sound? That's the sound of someone protecting herself from becoming a victim of identity theft. It only takes a minute to shred papers with personal information, but it can save you years of stress and worry.

Identity theft is the number one crime in the United States, with 10 million cases reported this year. Don't become the next victim. To find out how you can stay safe, call the Identity Theft Helpline at . . .

UNIT 3: Endurance Test

2A. LISTENING ONE: *Ultrarunner Jay Batchen*

Jay Batchen: . . . I mean, you're sleeping in a tent every night, there are sandstorms, you're sharing the tent with eight other people, it's not fully enclosed, so you have wind and sand and people snoring and rustling next to you. You're sleeping on rocks.

Tim Bourquin: Well, you know Jay, it doesn't sound like a whole lot of fun, so, you know, in the night, you're not getting a lot of sleep. What is in it for you? What does the race do for you personally?

LISTEN FOR MAIN IDEAS

Tim Bourquin: Thank you for joining us at EnduranceRadio.com. We've got another great interview for you today. We're going to be speaking with Jay Batchen. He was the first American to finish the Marathon des Sables. We're going to hear about that and his background in ultra running and a little bit about his background in endurance sports in general. So, Jay, thanks very much for joining us. I appreciate you taking the time to talk to us on the phone.

Jay Batchen: Thank you, Tim. It's my pleasure.

Tim Bourquin: So, talk about the Marathon des Sables. How did you get into that?

Jay Batchen: It's funny how I did get into the Marathon des Sables. I was introduced to it while working for the Discovery Channel. I filmed the event in 1999, which is actually the year my wife, Lisa Smith-Batchen, won the event. And that's how I ended up in Morocco and ended up learning about the event myself.

Tim Bourquin: So, did you know Lisa before that event, or you met her there?

Jay Batchen: Met her there.

Tim Bourquin: OK, so you ended up marrying the winner of the race that you were filming.

Jay Batchen: Yep.

Tim Bourquin: Oh, very good. So, talk about that race. How did that start? How long is it? Where is it? That sort of thing, for our listeners that may not know.

Jay Batchen: Sure. The race is . . . it takes place in the Sahara Desert in southern Morocco, just outside of the Atlas Mountains. And the course is different every year. For instance, this year, it was a hundred and fifty-four mile course, and the year I ran it, in 2000, it was about a hundred and forty-eight that year, so . . .

Tim Bourquin: Wow.

Jay Batchen: . . . it just changes year to year, and obviously the terrain will change as well, since the course does.

Tim Bourquin: Now, is this a stage race, or is it just start, and go 'til you finish?

Jay Batchen: No, this particular race is a stage race, and the format is fairly, fairly similar each year, in that the first three stages are all around 20 miles, give or take, and then the fourth stage is a 50 mile, ah, long stage. Then that's followed by a full marathon. And the last day basically makes up the difference, just gets you back into a town, and it's a little shorter. Gives everyone a chance to get across the finish line and get back to the small town where we rendezvous and clean up for a nice night of awards and festivities.

Tim Bourquin: If you're able to stay standing at that point, I guess.

Jay Batchen: Definitely. And what's unique about this race is that you do have to carry all of your food, extra clothing, um, and things like that for the entire event. You are given a ration of water each day at checkpoints roughly about six to eight miles in length.

I mean, you're sleeping in a tent every night, there are sandstorms, you're sharing the tent with eight other people, it's not fully enclosed, so you have wind and sand and people snoring and rustling next to you. You're sleeping on rocks.

Tim Bourquin: Well, you know Jay, it doesn't sound like a whole lot of fun, so, you know, in the night, you're not getting a lot of sleep. What is in it for you? What does the race do for you personally?

Jay Batchen: That's a good question, and it's a question that many people ask. And what I tell them is, that this race is more than a race. It's a life experience. And what I mean by that is: you're sharing a tent with eight other people, and you're going through the same highs and lows every day. It might not be at the same time, but you're running in the same heat, you're running in the same wind, you're sleeping in the same sandstorms on the cold nights, and for me it's about meeting the other people that are running this event, and sharing stories with them and sharing the experience with them. And it's so hard to describe to someone who hasn't been there and run the event. So for me, it's completing the distance and knowing that I can do it, feeling that I can do it, but it's meeting the people from all over the world, from all walks of life, and just sharing it with them that makes it special.

LISTEN FOR DETAILS

(Repeat Listen for Main Ideas)

MAKE INFERENCES

Excerpt One

Jay Batchen: . . . I filmed the event in 1999, which is actually the year my wife, Lisa Smith-Batchen, won the event. And that's how I ended up in Morocco and ended up learning about the event myself.

Tim Bourquin: So, did you know Lisa before that event, or you met her there?

Jay Batchen: Met her there.

Tim Bourquin: OK, so you ended up marrying the winner of the race that you were filming.

Jay Batchen: Yep.

Tim Bourquin: Oh, very good.

Excerpt Two

Jay Batchen: . . . the format is fairly, fairly similar each year, in that the first three stages are all around twenty miles, give or take, and then the fourth stage is a fifty mile, ah, long stage. Then that's followed by a full marathon. And the last day basically makes up the difference, just gets you back into a town, and it's a little shorter. Gives everyone a chance to get across the finish line and get back to the small town where we rendezvous and clean up for a nice night of awards and festivities.

Tim Bourquin: If you're able to stay standing at that point, I guess.

Jay Batchen: Definitely.

Excerpt Three

Jay Batchen: I mean, you're sleeping in a tent every night, there are sandstorms, you're sharing the tent with eight other people, it's not fully enclosed, so you have wind and sand and people snoring and rustling next to you. You're sleeping on rocks.

Tim Bourquin: Well, you know Jay, it doesn't sound like a whole lot of fun, so, you know, in the night, you're not getting a lot of sleep.

2B. LISTENING TWO: *Sports Psychology*

Professor: So last time, when we were discussing the growth of endurance sports, a question came up about the motivation for getting into these sports. Why would anyone want to go through so much physical pain and stress? What's in it for them? Well, looking at the research, there are a couple points that seem especially important:

One of these is the personality of endurance athletes. As a group, these people tend to be high achievers, you know, people who set high goals for themselves—both in sports and in life in general. They like difficult challenges, and they aren't happy with goals that are easy to achieve. So endurance sports fits right into this type of personality. These sports are very difficult, very extreme—like ultramarathons where people run hundreds of miles, often in extreme heat or cold—but the athletes get a lot of satisfaction from it. And when setting goals, most endurance athletes don't focus on winning the race. Instead, they have personal goals, like maybe just finishing the race is enough, or finishing with a better time than before. So it's really more about the athletes challenging themselves, doing their personal best, and always pushing to do better.

Another source of motivation is the relationship between the athletes. In general, endurance athletes don't see the other athletes in a race as opponents, or people they're trying to beat. Instead, they see them as partners—partners in this unique adventure, doing something that no one else is doing. They share the highs and lows of the race, the pain and the pleasure, and they feel that they are in the experience together. And the athletes report this as a life changing experience . . . an emotional high that keeps them wanting to come back for more. So this, this, strong emotional experience is a big part of the motivation.

UNIT 4: Separated by the Same Language

2A. LISTENING ONE: *Accent and Identity*

Peter: . . . Also, whenever I opened my mouth I could see people thinking, "I wonder where he's from," and that would be the first question: "Where are you from?" And then I'd have to go into this long explanation about my background . . . I got tired of it.

LISTEN FOR MAIN IDEAS

Lisa: Hi. This is Lisa. I'm doing a project on accents for my sociolinguistics course, so I'm interviewing some of my friends from grad school. This is my friend Peter. Peter, can you give me a little background on where you grew up?

Peter: I'm from St. Vincent, in the Caribbean. That's what we call home. And I've lived in the States, here in North Carolina, for six years.

Lisa: So do you feel that you have an accent?

Peter: Well, I wasn't aware of my accent until I came here. Obviously, growing up in St. Vincent, no one told me I had an accent because we all spoke the same.

Lisa: So, how did you feel about your accent when you came here?

Peter: Well, when I came here, many people commented on my accent. So I started to be aware of it. I still get comments all the time. I mean they always say, things . . . things like . . .

Lisa: Like? Like, what do they say?

Peter: Oh, just, I mean, people say, "Oh, I love your accent. It's so musical. Keep talking."

Lisa: So, you're saying that they like your accent?

Peter: Yes, but I also remember—when I first came—I felt that I spoke so slowly, everyone else spoke much faster. . . . Some people stereotyped me because of that. I could tell that they were thinking, "He's not very bright." You know, "He speaks so slowly," you know, "so he must be thinking slowly, too." So that made me feel pretty self-conscious. Also, whenever I opened my mouth I could see people thinking, "I wonder where he's from," and that would be the first question: "Where are you from?" And then I'd have to go into this long explanation about my background . . . I got tired of it.

Lisa: But wasn't that a good way to meet people?

Peter: Hmm. Maybe. . . . But there's a difference between meeting people and making friends. I mean . . . here I was, a first-year student, meeting lots of people, but I always felt that the other students didn't really understand who I was. It made me feel like . . . like I didn't fit in.

Lisa: So did you try to fit in?

Peter: Yeah, I did. Not intentionally. It's funny how that happens, but I'd hear myself saying, "first" instead of "furst."

Lisa: Oh, OK . . .

Peter: And I'd try to speak quickly. Oh . . . and I'd try to use the slang that everyone else used. A lot of the slang was different . . .

Lisa: But . . . but you don't have an American accent now. What happened?

Peter: Well, I started to feel differently when I moved to the International House.

Lisa: The International House?

Peter: Yes, this house on campus where foreign students lived. I started going to parties there and I really felt like I fit in because everyone had a different accent. They didn't stereotype me, and everyone accepted everyone else's accent. Hmm . . . I guess that's the main thing. When people accept you, then you can speak the way you want.

Lisa: I see . . . So do you think your accent has changed at all?

Peter: It's really strange because I go back home, and my friends say to me, "But Peter, you lived abroad all these years and you don't even have an American accent! You speak exactly the same!"

Lisa: So it sounds like you want to keep your accent.

Peter: I do now. It's part of who I am . . . part of my identity. But of course, you know, I'm also older now. I'm not trying to fit in with a crowd, so I'm comfortable with the way I speak.

LISTEN FOR DETAILS

(Repeat Listen for Main Ideas)

MAKE INFERENCES

Excerpt One

Peter: I'm from St. Vincent, in the Caribbean. That's what we call home. And I've lived in the States, here in North Carolina, for six years.

Lisa: So do you feel that you have an accent?

Peter: Well, I wasn't aware of my accent until I came here. Obviously, growing up in St. Vincent, no one told me I had an accent because we all spoke the same.

Excerpt Two

Peter: . . . I also remember—when I first came—I felt that I spoke so slowly, everyone else spoke much faster. . . . Some people stereotyped me because of that. I could tell that they were thinking, "He's not very bright." You know, "He speaks so slowly," you know, "so he must be thinking slowly, too." So that made me feel pretty self-conscious. Also, whenever I opened my mouth I could see people thinking, "I wonder where he's from," and that would be the first question: "Where are you from?" And then I'd have to go into this long explanation about my background . . . I got tired of it.

Excerpt Three

Peter: . . . It's really strange because I go back home, and my friends say to me, "But Peter, you lived abroad all these years and you don't even have an American accent! You speak exactly the same!"

Lisa: So it sounds like you want to keep your accent.

Peter: I do now. It's part of who I am . . . part of my identity. But of course, you know, I'm also older now. I'm not trying to fit in with a crowd, so I'm comfortable with the way I speak.

2B.   LISTENING TWO: *Code-Switching*

Professor: OK. So, let's get back to the idea of code-switching, which I mentioned earlier. Now, code-switching is when a person switches—changes—from one language or dialect to another. So someone may speak one way at work or school, but another way at home or with friends. Basically, they switch languages or dialects depending on where they are and who they're talking to.

So, one example of code-switching—changing dialects—is the way teenagers change their speech when talking to their friends versus talking to an adult. A lot of teenagers speak a "teen dialect"—which is a dialect used by teenagers with a *lot* of slang . . . slang their parents don't understand—and usually hate too, right? Like, they are saying: "Why are you talking like that? What are you saying?"

But when kids switch between this teen dialect and the standard dialect, this is code-switching. So, let me give you an example. Let's say a teenager is leaving the house and he says to his friend: "Gotta bounce. We gotta meet the crew." Then his dad asks, "Hey, where're you going?" and the kid says, "We have to go. We're meeting our friends downtown." So he's saying the same thing to both people, but with his friends, he's using a teen dialect, "Gotta bounce" meaning "We have to go" and "the crew" for "my friends." And he's code-switching when he switches from the teen dialect into standard English with his dad.

Alright, so why do teenagers use this kind of teen dialect? Well, because it's an important way for teens to show their identity—to show that they fit in with their friends. It also shows that they're separate from their parents. So by code-switching into a teen dialect with their friends, a teen is saying, "I'm one of you." . . . and saying to their parents, "I'm not like you."

3C.   SPEAKING

PRONUNCIATION: *Can / Can't*

Exercise 1

1. She can't take that class.
2. He can speak French.
3. I can't understand American slang.
4. We can speak that dialect.
5. I can't recognize his accent.
6. She can't fit in.
7. I can comment on that.
8. She invited me to come. I said that I can.

UNIT 5: Culture and Commerce

2A.   LISTENING ONE: *Tourist Attraction or Human Zoo?*

Reporter: Each year around 10,000 tourists visit three small villages along the Thai/Myanmar border to see the famous long-necked women. The attraction is a tradition that requires women to stretch their necks by wearing brass coils. Originally from the Pa Daung tribe, the women and their families came from Myanmar to Thailand in the 1980s to escape poverty and war. Their new lives are very different from their lives as farmers in Myanmar. Now they make a living talking with tourists, posing for pictures, and selling handmade souvenirs.

LISTEN FOR MAIN IDEAS

Announcer: Critics call it "a human zoo." Tour companies consider it a tourist attraction. Whichever the case, the long-necked women of Pa Daung have become an important source of money for several small villages on the border of Thailand and Myanmar. Reporter Mike Danforth has this report.

Tour Leader: Welcome to Nai Soi. Please buy your ticket here.

Reporter: Each year around 10,000 tourists visit three small villages along the Thai/Myanmar border to see the famous long-necked women. The attraction is a tradition that requires women to stretch their necks by wearing brass coils. Originally from the Pa Daung tribe, the women and their families came from Myanmar to Thailand in the 1980s to escape poverty and war. Their new lives are very different from their lives as farmers in Myanmar. Now they make a living talking with tourists, posing for pictures, and selling handmade souvenirs.

When a Pa Daung girl turns five, a thick coil of brass is wrapped around her neck. Throughout her life, more coils are added until her neck carries up to 25 brass rings, weighing up to 22 pounds. The coils push up her chin and press down her collarbone, making her neck longer. Pa Peiy, a young woman with 20 neck rings, describes her early years of neck stretching:

Pa Peiy: At first it was painful, but now it's OK. Now sleeping, eating, working . . . everything is OK, but I cannot take it off . . . so this is my life.

Reporter: It truly *is* her life. Pa Peiy's neck is now so weak that if she takes off the coils, her head will fall forward and she will stop breathing. Despite the discomfort, Pa Daung women in Thailand continue to wear the coils even though the tradition has almost disappeared in Myanmar. Why? Because there's money in it. Ma Nang, a graceful woman with 24 neck rings explains:

Ma Nang: In Myanmar I worked hard growing food. Now I sit and tourists take pictures. In one month I get 70 to 80 dollars. It's easy, and it's good money for my family. Sometimes I'm tired of tourists always looking . . . but it's good money.

Reporter: Each year, as the long-necked women have become more and more popular, the controversy about them has increased. In an outdoor restaurant near Nai Soi, tourists discuss whether or not to visit the village. Sandra, a Canadian woman, feels that it's fine to visit.

Sandra: I don't really see a problem. I mean this is their tradition . . . and so if I go, it's like I'm helping them to preserve it. Spending my money is also helping them. You know, they make a living from tourism, so they need us.

Reporter: Fredrick, from Germany, feels differently.

Fredrick: Actually, I don't see that we're preserving tradition at all. This tradition has died in Myanmar already. These women are just hurting their bodies to entertain us. It's like paying to go see animals in a zoo. It's degrading.

Reporter: For now, the future of the long-necked women is easy to predict. As long as there are tourists who will pay to see them, they will continue to wrap their daughters' necks. The controversy continues, with one side seeing the villages as examples of how tourism can save dying traditions, and others criticizing it as harmful and degrading to the Pa Daung women.

LISTEN FOR DETAILS

(Repeat Listen for Main Ideas)

MAKE INFERENCES

Excerpt One

Pa Peiy: At first it was painful, but now it's OK. Now sleeping, eating, working . . . everything is OK, but I cannot take it off . . . so this is my life.

Excerpt Two

Ma Nang: In Myanmar I worked hard growing food. Now I sit and tourists take pictures. In one month I get 70 to 80 dollars. It's easy, and it's good money for my family. Sometimes I'm tired of tourists always looking . . . but it's good money.

Excerpt Three

Sandra: I don't really see a problem. I mean this is their tradition . . . and so if I go, it's like I'm helping them to preserve it. Spending my money is also helping them. You know, they make a living from tourism, so they need us.

Excerpt Four

Fredrick: Actually, I don't see that we're preserving tradition at all. This tradition has died in Myanmar already. These women are just hurting their bodies to entertain us. It's like paying to go see animals in a zoo. It's degrading.

2B. LISTENING TWO: *Town Hall Meeting in Cape Cod*

Mayor: OK. We're here today to talk about tourism in our community. Let's start with the first item on our agenda—identifying some of the problems caused by the increasing number of tourists we get every year.

Woman 1: Well, for one, the traffic is just terrible in the summer! In winter, it takes me about 15 minutes to drive into town. But in the summer, it can be 45 minutes or more. It's ridiculous!

Man 1: I agree, traffic gets bad, but in my mind, the biggest problem is housing. The cost of buying or renting a home here is way too high! Yeah! It's just too expensive on a regular salary. Too many homes are sold as vacation homes for rich people. And that leaves nothing for the working people who live here. I mean I own a seafood restaurant, OK? And I've got a waitress who's living in her car right now because she can't afford any other place to live. We've got to do something about that!

Woman 2: Can I say something? OK, I know it's difficult to have all these tourists around during the summer, but I, for one, am very happy to have them. I run a souvenir shop, and I do about 80 percent of my business for the year in the summer. And I'm not the only one. Tourists are the lifeblood of our community. Without them, I wouldn't be able to make a living. We've got to keep them coming.

Man 2: Of course we need the tourists, no one's denying that. But I'm a business owner, too, and one problem I see is that we depend on the weather so much. When it rains, tourists don't come, huh? This season has been really difficult for my business 'cause of that. With all this rain last month, I lost a lot of money because people weren't coming in the door. I'd like to see us develop where we don't depend on the weather so much.

Mayor: OK, before we move on, I'd like to address one of the comments made here . . .

UNIT 6: The Art of Storytelling

2A. LISTENING ONE: *Lavender*

Robert and David were good friends. Late one spring evening, they were driving to a spring social. As they drove along the road, Robert and David both realized that they didn't have dates! So David said to Robert, "Some good friend you are. What happened to our dates for the evening?"

"Oh, I'm sorry. I just couldn't get them to go."

"Well, we'll find dates at the dance. There'll be lots of girls there without partners."

As they drove along the road, the headlights fell on someone walking along the side of the highway.

LISTEN FOR MAIN IDEAS

Robert and David were good friends. Late one spring evening, they were driving to a spring social. As they drove along the road, Robert and David both realized that they didn't have dates! So David said to Robert, "Some good friend you are. What happened to our dates for the evening?"

"Oh, I'm sorry. I just couldn't get them to go."

"Well, we'll find dates at the dance. There'll be lots of girls there without partners."

As they drove along the road, the headlights fell on someone walking along the side of the highway. As they approached the person walking, they could see that it was a young girl, dressed in a lavender evening dress. Robert looked at David, David looked at Robert, and they both smiled. They slowed the car down, and when they stopped, they said to the young woman, "We're on our way to the social."

"Oh," she said, "so am I!"

"Would you like to ride?"

"I would indeed," she said.

She got into the back of the car. Robert and David introduced themselves and she said, "I'm Lavender, just like my dress. Just call me Lavender."

As they drove along, they decided that they would be together that night. At the dance, Robert danced with Lavender, David danced with Lavender, and as the evening wore on, the spring air turned a little cool. And Robert said to Lavender, "Are you cold? Would you like my coat?"

"Oh, yes," she said, "I am just a bit chilled."

And Robert said, "I think it's raining outside. Could we drive you home?"

"Oh, yes," she said, "Thank you. I didn't want to walk on the highway alone tonight."

And as they started down the highway, Lavender explained that both her mom and dad were just a little strict. And it would be very difficult to explain how she had come home with two strange young men. So it would be easier to stop at the edge of the driveway and she could walk to the house without any explanation to her parents. And Robert and David understood. And as they stopped at the edge of the driveway, Lavender got out, blew them a kiss from the tip of her fingers, and walked down the driveway and through the trees toward the house. And then they realized that she still had the coat! David said, "Tomorrow. We'll get it back tomorrow. That will be the excuse we use to come and visit."

Early the next morning, David and Robert were on the highway, driving toward the house. But as they drove up and down the highway, they couldn't seem to find the driveway.

"It was here!"

"No, it was over there!"

"It was here," said Robert, "but look, it's all grown up. There're weeds, and grass, and rocks. It wasn't grown up last night! But this is the driveway . . . you see, there's a house between the trees."

So they stopped the car and got out, and walked along the driveway. And as they cleared the trees, they could see the house. And Robert said to David, "Are you sure that we're in the right place? Look at this house. Look at the windows—they're all broken! And look how the door hangs from the hinges! This couldn't be the place!" They walked to the back of the house. And there, in a little picket fence, was a little family cemetery with five, six, seven gravestones. And hanging on one of the gravestones, a middle-sized gravestone, was the coat. And as they lifted the coat from the stone they both said, "Aaah!"

The name on the gravestone was "Lavender." They had spent the evening with a ghost. And that's the end of that!

LISTEN FOR DETAILS

(Repeat Listen for Main Ideas)

MAKE INFERENCES

Excerpt One

. . . And Robert said to Lavender, "Are you cold? Would you like my coat?"

"Oh, yes," she said, "I am just a bit chilled."

And Robert said, "I think it's raining outside. Could we drive you home?"

"Oh, yes," she said, "Thank you. I didn't want to walk on the highway alone tonight."

Excerpt Two

. . . But as they drove up and down the highway, they couldn't seem to find the driveway.

"It was here!"

"No, it was over there!"

"It was here," said Robert, "but look, it's all grown up. There're weeds, and grass, and rocks. It wasn't grown up last night! But this is the driveway . . . you see, there's a house between the trees."

Excerpt Three

. . . They walked to the back of the house. And there, in a little picket fence, was a little family cemetery with five, six, seven gravestones. And hanging on one of the gravestones, a middle-sized gravestone, was the coat. And as they lifted the coat from the stone they both said, "Aaah!"

The name on the gravestone was "Lavender."

2B. LISTENING TWO: *How to Tell a Story*

People often ask me: "What's the secret to telling a great story?" And I tell them this: Remember that telling a story is much more than just saying the words. It's what you DO with the words that brings the story to life.

Like using your voice. You can change the feeling of a story just by changing the way you speak. So let's say, I'm telling a story about a bear that's chasing a little boy . . . . And I want to give the feeling of the chase, of the little boy being so afraid. So, I can start talking faster and louder. "The bear was close behind the boy, and the boy started running, and the bear started running, and the boy was running faster and faster, so fast he could barely breathe, but still the bear got closer and closer and CLOSER!" See how I started talking faster and louder? That makes the story more exciting.

And if I wanted to make the story SCARY I could speak slowly and softly: "And the little boy . . . heard a noise behind him . . . and turned around to see the bear . . . looking over . . . his shoulder."

So, it's not *what* I'm saying, but *how* I'm saying it that makes the difference.

Also, remember that dialogue is very important in storytelling. Don't just tell your audience what happened, but bring the characters to life with dialogue.

For example, don't tell them: "The bear told the little boy to stop running."

Show them what he said: "Stop running!" said the bear.

And you can also use your voice to create different characters. For example, the little boy might talk in a high, squeaky voice like this: "Oh please Mr. Bear. Please, please, don't eat me!" And the bear might talk in a low, growly voice, like this: "Don't worry little boy. I don't want to hurt you." So using these different voices is more fun to listen to, but also helps your audience understand which character is talking, so they don't get confused.

So by playing with your voice, using your voice in different ways, you can really have fun with the story and make it much more exciting and interesting for your audience.

2C. INTEGRATE LISTENINGS ONE AND TWO

STEP 1: Organize

(Repeat Make Inferences)

3C. SPEAKING

PRONUNCIATION: *Rhythm of Prepositional Phrases*

Exercise 1

1. Robert and David drove from their house.
2. Lavender was waiting on the road.
3. She walked with Robert.
4. The three friends went to the dance.
5. They got back in the car.
6. Robert and David were looking at the coat in the backyard.
7. Robert pointed to the gravestone.
8. They ran for the car.

Exercise 2

1. come to dinner   come tomorrow
2. Thanks for getting a job.   Hank's forgetting his job.
3. It's hard to dance.   It's cold today.
4. a fortune at school   a fortunate school
5. at nine   arrive
6. point at Tom   pointed top

UNIT 7: Voluntary Simplicity

2A. LISTENING ONE: *Urban Homesteaders*

Karen Brown: A group of chickens are walking around the backyard of Daniel Staub, Kristin Brennan, and their two young children. The chickens lay about 10 eggs a day. In their garden, vegetables are starting to grow. And when their kids want something sweet, they go out back and get honey from a beehive.

Kristin Brennan: There was this one hive, and they produced 80 pounds of honey this year, that we actually harvested. And then this . . .

Karen Brown: Brennan and Staub are both 31 years old and college educated. Two years ago, they began a homesteading experiment. Now, they try to live a self-sufficient lifestyle.

LISTEN FOR MAIN IDEAS

Karen Brown: A group of chickens are walking around the backyard of Daniel Staub, Kristin Brennan, and their two young children. The chickens lay about 10 eggs a day. In their garden, vegetables are starting to grow. And when their kids want something sweet, they go out back and get honey from a beehive.

Kristin Brennan: There was this one hive, and they produced 80 pounds of honey this year, that we actually harvested. And then this . . .

Karen Brown: Brennan and Staub are both 31 years old and college educated. Two years ago, they began a homesteading experiment. Now, they try to live a self-sufficient lifestyle. They produce almost all of their own food instead of shopping at the supermarket. They wear used clothes and shop at secondhand stores. They have no car, and instead bike, walk, or take the bus, whether they're going around town or visiting family in the next state. They don't use electricity in their house, either. They have candles for light and heat their home with wood.

Daniel Staub: We are attempting to live within a local economy. Locally-based economy is really about community for me, and it's about connection between people and each other, and the natural world around them.

Karen Brown: There is a long tradition of homesteading in the United States, but most homesteaders live in rural areas, on farms and in the countryside. What makes Brennan and Staub's lifestyle different is that they live in the middle of a poor, inner city neighborhood in Springfield, Massachusetts. They hope that other people will notice their simple lifestyle, and consider changing their own habits.

Daniel Staub: We could live this way anywhere. The question is, in what way will we be offering it most to people? A lot of people in a lot of different situations can benefit from changing their consumption habits.

Karen Brown: Since their move, they've worked hard to build relationships with neighbors. And they've gotten especially close to local children.

Kristin Brennan: OK, so, you want to get as much of the root as you possibly can, so let me show you, LJ.

LJ: Like this?

Kristin Brennan: No. You want to first . . .

Karen Brown: Ten year old Lorenzo Nicholson is helping Brennan move plants from one part of the garden to another.

Kristin Brennan: . . . and you're gonna actually put your foot on top of the shovel.

LJ: I know.

Kristin Brennan: OK?

Karen Brown: Lorenzo is one of the young neighbors who enjoy spending most sunny afternoons in this backyard. However, the adults are harder to convince. Staub often tells family and friends that, even though it's more work, they enjoy their life this way. For instance, today they are sawing wood to burn in their wood stove.

Daniel Staub: If you see it as time that is taken away from, you know, something else that you really need to be doing, well, then it seems totally insane. But if you see it as something that is an activity worth doing in and of itself . . . you're getting exercise, you're spending time with family, you know, you're not using the fossil fuels that would be involved in using a chainsaw.

Karen Brown: While Brennan and Staub both believe in what they're doing, they still talk about how far to go. Brennan is usually more willing than her husband to put more wood on the fire when the house gets cold. And with two small children, she admits that she sometimes wants to use the clothes dryer that came with the house.

Kristin Brennan: And we've been tempted to throw diapers and covers into the dryer.

Karen Brown: And what stops you just before you do that?

Kristin Brennan: Well, I guess it's a slippery slope. We use the dryer once, maybe we would be lured by the dryer again, and so, we decided not to do it.

Karen Brown: However, neither Brennan nor Staub want to end their homesteading lifestyle. In fact, they hope to do more. Next year, they plan to buy a goat so they can have fresh milk. I'm Karen Brown.

LISTEN FOR DETAILS

(Repeat Listen for Main Ideas)

MAKE INFERENCES

Excerpt One

Karen Brown: Brennan and Staub are both 31 years old and college educated. Two years ago, they began a homesteading experiment. Now, they try to live a self-sufficient lifestyle. They produce almost all of their own food instead of shopping at the supermarket. They wear used clothes and shop at secondhand stores.

Daniel Staub: We are attempting to live within a local economy. Locally-based economy is really about community for me, and it's about connection between people and each other, and the natural world around them.

Excerpt Two

Karen Brown: . . . Staub often tells family and friends that, even though it's more work, they enjoy their life this way. For instance, today they are sawing wood to burn in their wood stove.

Daniel Staub: If you see it as time that is taken away from, you know, something else that you really need to be doing, well, then it seems totally insane. But if you see it as something that is an activity worth doing in and of itself . . . you're getting exercise, you're spending time with family, you know, you're not using the fossil fuels that would be involved in using a chainsaw.

Excerpt Three

Karen Brown: Brennan is usually more willing than her husband to put more wood on the fire when the house gets cold. And with two small children, she admits that she sometimes wants to use the clothes dryer that came with the house.

Kristin Brennan: And we've been tempted to throw diapers and covers into the dryer.

Karen Brown: And what stops you just before you do that?

Kristin Brennan: Well, I guess it's a slippery slope. We use the dryer once, maybe we would be lured by the dryer again, and so, we decided not to do it.

2B. LISTENING TWO: *Simple Gifts*

Exercise 2

Singer: Thank you. Thank you.

This next song is called "Simple Gifts." And was written by a man named Joseph Brackett. And you might know he was a Shaker. And if you know anything about Shakers, then it makes perfect sense that he would write this song.

And even though he wrote it a long time ago, it still has an important message for us today. How many times are we dragged down by all the stuff in our lives? All the stuff we own . . . all the things that we worry about . . . Well, this song reminds us that there is joy in simple things . . . joy in simple gifts . . .

'Tis the gift to be simple, 'tis the gift to be free,
'Tis the gift to come down where we ought to be,
And when we find ourselves in the place just right,
'Twill be in the valley of love and delight.

When true simplicity is gained,
To bow and to bend we shan't be ashamed,
To turn, turn will be our delight,
'Til by turning, turning we come 'round right.

When true simplicity is gained,
To bow and to bend we shan't be ashamed,
To turn, turn will be our delight,
'Til by turning, turning we come 'round right.

Exercise 3

(Repeat Exercise 2)

UNIT 8: Before You Say "I Do"

2A. LISTENING ONE: *A Prenuptial Agreement*

Host: Welcome to *Living Today,* the show that examines modern day issues that touch our daily lives. Today we'll be talking about marriage and how to prepare for that big step of actually tying the knot. When most couples marry, they discuss some important issues in advance, like how many children they want or where they want to live, but most of the day-to-day details and problems of married life are worked out after the wedding. Not so with my guests today, Steve and Karen Parsons, who have a 15-page marriage contract that states the rules they must follow in almost every aspect of their married life. So, Steve, Karen, welcome to the show.

LISTEN FOR MAIN IDEAS

Host: Welcome to *Living Today,* the show that examines modern day issues that touch our daily lives. Today we'll be talking about marriage and how to prepare for that big step of actually tying the knot. When most couples marry, they discuss some important issues in advance, like how many children they want or where they want to live, but most of the day-to-day details and problems of married life are worked out after the wedding. Not so with my guests today, Steve and Karen Parsons, who have a 15-page marriage contract that states the rules they must follow in almost every aspect of their married life. So, Steve, Karen, welcome to the show.

Steve: Thanks.

Karen: Nice to be here.

Host: So, I'd like to start off by asking you what *everybody* is probably wondering: Why did you decide to write this agreement? I mean, you've both been married before, am I right?

Steve: Yeah. I've been married twice, and Karen was married once before.

Karen: And so we have some experience about what goes wrong in a marriage.

Steve: Right.

Host: OK. And that's why you wrote this contract?

Karen: Right.

Steve: Yes, we found that most problems happen because the spouses have different expectations about the marriage. We wanted to talk about everything openly and honestly, you know, before we started living together as man and wife.

Karen: Yeah. For example, everyone has their quirks, and we're all bothered by things that might not seem important to someone else. Like, it used to really bother me when my ex-husband left his dirty clothes on the floor, so we put that in the contract: "Dirty clothing must be put in the laundry bag." And now Steve knows what my expectations are . . .

Steve: I'll say.

Karen: . . . and he won't be leaving HIS clothes on the floor, right sweetie?

Steve: Right.

Host: Well, I'm sure that some people hearing this report will think that this isn't very romantic.

Steve: Oh no. We disagree.

Karen: Actually, we think it's very romantic.

Steve: Yeah. It shows that we sat down and talked and really tried to understand each other. A lot of problems occur in a marriage because people don't open up and talk about what they want.

Karen: That's so true! Now, when we disagree about something, we work out a compromise that's good for both of us. You know, I'd much rather do that than get some "romantic" gift like flowers or candy.

Host: OK, so . . . I have to say some of these rules sound like . . . like, well, a business agreement. Many of them concern money in some way . . . even the ones about having children. Let's see. Right here, you say: "After our first child is born, the partner who makes less money will quit his or her job and stay home with the child." Well now, that's an interesting way to decide who will do the childcare!

Steve: Yeah, it's unusual, but it really makes sense. We definitely want someone home with our kids . . .

Karen: Oh yeah.

Steve: . . . and if Karen is the main breadwinner at that point, why should she stop working? It'll be better for all of us if I stay home.

Karen: Yeah. And the reason that we put in so many rules about money is that, in our experience, a lot of problems are caused by arguments about money.

Steve: Oh yeah.

Karen: So we decided to make a budget every year. And we put that in the contract, too.

Host: Hmm, well, I'm curious, do you spend a lot of time checking up on each other to see if the rules are being followed?

Karen: No, not at all. And we don't argue about them, either.

Steve: No. As a matter of fact, I think we spend less time arguing than most couples because we both know what the other person expects.

Karen: Yeah, and we can spend our time doing things we enjoy and just being with each other.

Host: What happens if one of you breaks a rule?

Steve: So far, that hasn't been a problem.

Karen: No. Hasn't happened.

Steve: Because we've agreed on them already.

Host: But what if, say . . . alright, here it says "Karen will cook the meals . . ." What if you don't want to cook dinner one night? What happens?

Steve: Well, we'll work something out. Maybe there's a good reason, like she's sick or something. We can still be flexible.

Host: OK. But what if it happens all the time . . .

Karen: Well, then we have to ask: Is this marriage really working? Because, let's face it, if we can't follow our own agreement, there's no point.

Host: Very true. So it sounds like you two are happy with this contract. Now let me ask you, do you think other couples should follow your example, and write marriage contracts of their own?

Steve: Well, it's a lot of work to write something like this . . .

Karen: That's for sure.

Steve: . . . but I think it could be useful to a lot of people.

Karen: Yeah, and you know, I bet there'd be fewer divorces.

Host: OK, well look, I know we have a lot of people waiting to get in on this discussion, so let's go to some calls. Hi, you're on the air. What do you think?

LISTEN FOR DETAILS

(Repeat Listen for Main Ideas)

MAKE INFERENCES

Excerpt One

Steve: Yes, we found that most problems happen because the spouses have different expectations about the marriage. We wanted to talk about everything openly and honestly, you know, before we started living together as man and wife.

Karen: Yeah. For example, everyone has their quirks, and we're all bothered by things that might not seem important to someone else. Like, it used to really bother me when my ex-husband left his dirty clothes on the floor, so we put that in the contract: "Dirty clothing must be put in the laundry bag." And now Steve knows what my expectations are . . .

Steve: I'll say.

Karen: . . . and he won't be leaving HIS clothes on the floor, right sweetie?

Steve: Right.

Excerpt Two

Host: I'm sure that some people hearing this report will think that this isn't very romantic.

Steve: Oh no. We disagree.

Karen: Actually, we think it's very romantic.

Steve: Yeah. It shows that we sat down and talked and really tried to understand each other. A lot of problems occur in a marriage because people don't open up and talk about what they want.

Karen: That's so true! Now, when we disagree about something, we work out a compromise that's good for both of us. You know, I'd much rather do that than get some "romantic" gift like flowers or candy.

Excerpt Three

Host: I'm curious, do you spend a lot of time checking up on each other to see if the rules are being followed?

Karen: No, not at all. And we don't argue about them, either.

Steve: No. As a matter of fact, I think we spend less time arguing than most couples because we both know what the other person expects.

Karen: Yeah, and we can spend our time doing things we enjoy and just being with each other.

2B. LISTENING TWO: *Reactions to the Prenuptial Agreement*

Caller 1: I'm glad you guys are happy, but I'd never sign a prenuptial agreement like this. No way. I don't care what you say; it's just not very romantic. I mean if you really love someone, you don't need to write all these things down. You just need to learn how to make your spouse happy and you've got to work out your problems right when they come up.

Caller 2: I don't know about all this. . . . It might be a good idea, but the main problem is this contract has WAY too many details. Like the rule about going to sleep at 11:00 P.M. What if one person wasn't sleepy or wanted to watch the news or something? That would be breaking a rule, right? It's crazy. You can't plan every detail in your life. That's ridiculous!

Caller 3: Well I think it's a great idea! You know what? I bet there'd be a lot fewer divorces if everyone did this. Most couples don't know how to open up and talk about their problems. We've all seen it, right? They let small things bother them and they may or may not say anything at the time, and then they finally blow up and have a big fight. And then the problem gets worse 'cause they don't know how to say "I'm sorry" afterwards. I think a contract like this could be a really helpful way to teach couples how to talk about their problems.

Caller 4: I'm a lawyer, and I can tell you that this prenuptial agreement isn't a legal contract. It may look legal and everything, but it wouldn't hold up in court. Let's say a guy has a problem with his wife and he goes to court and he says, "I want a divorce because my wife didn't cook dinner . . . ." Well, the judge wouldn't give him a divorce for that, would he? No way! So, legally, this contract is just a bunch of words. It has no power.

Caller 5: Yeah. I know a lot of people might think that this contract idea is crazy, but I think . . . I think it could be useful to help couples decide if they really SHOULD get married. I mean, a lot of couples, when they get married they do it, you know, because they're all in love with the other person and so on. But they don't look carefully at who the person is, really. I mean, they rush into things without thinking. And I think this contract would make both people think a lot more carefully about their expectations and, you know if marriage is the right thing to do.

UNIT 9: Personal Carbon Footprint

2A. LISTENING ONE: *Personal Carbon Footprint*

Curt Nickisch: Carbon dioxide may be invisible, but looking around her house, Ellen Schoenfeld-Beeks sees it almost anywhere she looks, even in her morning tea. She knows those blue flames under the teapot are making carbon dioxide. So does the heat for her house. Even the TV uses electricity that comes from burning coal. All of them emit carbon dioxide, the most common greenhouse gas. Schoenfeld-Beeks feels guilty for contributing to global warming.

LISTEN FOR MAIN IDEAS

Curt Nickisch: Carbon dioxide may be invisible, but looking around her house, Ellen Schoenfeld-Beeks sees it almost anywhere she looks, even in her morning tea. She knows those blue flames under the teapot are making carbon dioxide. So does the heat for her house. Even the TV uses electricity that comes from burning coal. All of them emit carbon dioxide, the most common greenhouse gas. Schoenfeld-Beeks feels guilty for contributing to global warming.

Ellen Schoenfeld-Beeks: I also burn wood in my wood stove, and that doesn't make me feel any better, actually. Twenty years ago it did. I used to think, "Oh, this is cool. I'm not using any oil or gas," but you're still putting the carbon dioxide into the air, so . . . can't win . . . can't win . . .

Curt Nickisch: But now there may be a way. Schoenfeld-Beeks was one of the first people to log onto a new website and pay to offset her own carbon dioxide emissions. Here's how it works: She visited the website to first find out how much carbon dioxide she puts in the air each year. This is called her "Carbon Footprint."

Ellen Schoenfeld-Beeks: See, you need to find your electricity kilowatt hours per year, or you can choose household size, which means single family home.

Curt Nickisch: The website adds up her energy use, including the miles she's driven in her car and flown in an airplane. Then it estimates her "Carbon Footprint." Like the average American, Schoenfeld-Beeks adds about 20 tons of carbon dioxide to the atmosphere each year. She then paid $100 to programs that promise to take greenhouse gases back out—no more guilt. But Anton Finelli, who created the website, does not like that term, "guilt."

Anton Finelli: We should think of it in terms of personal responsibility for taking action to benefit the environment by reducing our personal climate footprint, our personal global warming impact.

Curt Nickisch: Finelli says factories and other businesses already pay to offset large amounts of carbon dioxide emissions. The money goes to programs that reduce greenhouse gasses. Finelli set up the website to let individuals make the same sort of payment.

Anton Finelli: The idea here is that while one transaction may be small, if there are millions of transactions, the effect will make a significant difference.

Curt Nickisch: Half the money collected at Finelli's website goes to a company he runs. It collects methane from landfills around the country. The other half goes to planting trees. Plants take carbon dioxide out of the air and use it to grow. It's not clear how many people will want to pay into programs such as these, says Rich Rosenzweig. He is the chief operating officer of NatSource. It's an international company that collects money from large businesses and sends it to programs that reduce greenhouse gas emissions. His company tried to offer this same service to individuals, but Rosenzweig's company did not get much business from them.

Rich Rosenzweig: At the end of the day, the public has to be willing to spend money on it. And although there, you know, there's interest, it would be a, you know, challenging business to start.

Curt Nickisch: For Anton Finelli, business has been slow. He hopes, though, that as people learn more about the problem of global warming, they may want to spend more money to solve it. A recent survey found that Americans think climate change is the country's most important environmental problem. One of those people, Ellen Schoenfeld-Beeks, is happy to be doing something.

Ellen Schoenfeld-Beeks: I don't know that it's the be all and end all of what people can do, I don't know how much this really makes a difference, but part of me feels like well, at least I'm trying.

Curt Nickisch: And at least she feels less guilty, she says, when she turns on the stove to heat her morning tea. I'm Curt Nickisch.

LISTEN FOR DETAILS

(Repeat Listen for Main Ideas)

MAKE INFERENCES

Excerpt One

Curt Nickisch: But Anton Finelli, who created the website, does not like that term, "guilt."

Anton Finelli: We should think of it in terms of personal responsibility for taking action to benefit the environment by reducing our personal climate footprint, our personal global warming impact.

Excerpt Two

Curt Nickisch: It's not clear how many people will want to pay into programs such as these, says Rich Rosenzweig.

Rich Rosenzweig: At the end of the day, the public has to be willing to spend money on it. And although there, you know, there's interest, it would be a, you know, challenging business to start.

Excerpt Three

Curt Nickisch: Ellen Schoenfeld-Beeks, is happy to be doing something.

Ellen Schoenfeld-Beeks: I don't know that it's the be all and end all of what people can do, I don't know how much this really makes a difference, but part of me feels like well, at least I'm trying.

2B. LISTENING TWO: *A Call to Action*

Exercise 1

Speaker: We are here today because we want to stop global warming. Like me, you're trying hard to reduce your own personal carbon footprint. And these small, individual changes do have an impact, do help lower our carbon emissions.

But it's not enough. It's not enough for individuals to change. We need governments to change. We need industry to change. We need big changes if we want to stop global warming from destroying our planet.

One third . . . one third of our global carbon emissions—35 percent—comes from producing electricity. We need government and industry to work together to lower these emissions. To develop new, cleaner technology to heat our homes, power our factories, and to keep the lights on.

Another 20 percent, 20 percent of our emissions comes from transportation. We need government and industry to work together to build more energy efficient cars and trucks. To build more public transportation. Good quality public transportation that will let us get rid of our cars and the pollution they produce forever!

Another 20 percent of all emissions comes from industry—our factories and businesses. Putting tons upon tons of carbon into the air . . . our air . . . every single minute. It's time to say *enough!* We need these businesses to lower their own personal carbon footprints!

So my message to you today is: keep trying to reduce your personal carbon footprint. But also stand up, stand up and demand . . . demand that government and industry do their part. Because that is what will really make a difference!

UNIT 10: To Spank or Not to Spank?

2A. LISTENING ONE: *The Spanking Debate*

Announcer: When a father was recently arrested at a shopping mall for spanking his child, it started a debate about corporal punishment. Is spanking an acceptable form of child discipline? Or is it a form of child abuse? Charles Dean has our report.

LISTEN FOR MAIN IDEAS

Announcer: When a father was recently arrested at a shopping mall for spanking his child, it started a debate about corporal punishment. Is spanking an acceptable form of child discipline? Or is it a form of child abuse? Charles Dean has our report.

Charles Dean: The case that has everyone talking is the arrest of Dale Clover in St. Louis, Missouri. Clover is a 36-year-old father of three. He was arrested when a store employee saw him spanking his five-year-old son. The employee called the police and Clover was arrested for child abuse. He admits that he hit his son, but says it was discipline, not abuse.

Around the country, parents have mixed feelings about spanking. Studies show that most parents—about 90 percent—say they've spanked their children at least once. But they also say that they don't like spanking and think it's NOT the best form of discipline.

Tyler Robinson is a father of four. He never spanks his children. He feels it sends the wrong message.

Tyler Robinson: I want my children to learn right from wrong, but not out of fear. Spanking teaches children to be afraid of their parents, not respect them. I want my children to think of me as a friend, you know, someone they can talk with about problems.

Charles Dean: Robinson also thinks it teaches kids to use violence to solve problems.

Tyler Robinson: That's not a lesson I want to teach my children. I don't want my kids to hit anyone, so I don't hit them. There are lots of other ways you can discipline your kids without hitting.

Charles Dean: Rhonda Moore disagrees. She has two young children. She thinks parents these days are too permissive and can't control their children. In her view, spanking is an effective form of discipline.

Rhonda Moore: It's a parent's job to set clear limits, and spanking helps kids understand those limits. It sends a clear message. You know, a little bit of pain teaches a child right from wrong. It's like burning your hand on a hot stove. Pain is nature's way of teaching us.

Charles Dean: Moore says there's a big difference between spanking and child abuse.

Rhonda Moore: Child abuse is done out of anger, when a parent loses control. Spanking is done out of love. Now, when I spank my kids, I always talk to them before and after, and explain why I'm spanking them. They understand that I'm doing this because I love them, not because I want to hurt them.

Charles Dean: Most doctors and psychologists disagree. Beverly Lau is a child psychologist. She says spanking isn't effective.

Beverly Lau: It may stop bad behavior in the short term 'cause the child's afraid of getting spanked again! But what happens when mom and dad aren't around? They just repeat the behavior, 'cause no one's there to stop them. Instead, parents should use other forms of discipline, to teach children to think about their actions and make the right choices, no matter who is watching.

Charles Dean: Instead of spanking, Dr. Lau advocates problem solving and consequences as better ways to teach children life lessons.

Beverly Lau: Children learn best by doing. The best way to teach them how to behave is to get them to say what they did wrong and to think of what they should've done instead. We call this active problem solving and we need to show our children how to do it. There still needs to be a consequence for the misbehavior. But it should be a consequence that makes sense. Like, "you hit your friend so we need to leave the playground." Or, "you didn't finish your homework so you can't watch TV."

Charles Dean: Dr. Lau highlights another problem with spanking. It can easily turn into abuse.

Beverly Lau: As a parent, it can be very hard to control your anger. If you're hitting your child, and you're angry, it's too easy to get carried away and hit too hard. So there's a danger there.

Charles Dean: Whether or not you approve of spanking, some see legal problems with arresting parents. John Simmons is a family law attorney.

John Simmons: Parents know their children best. They know the best way to discipline them. Do we really want the government to control what we do in our own families? Parents have the right to decide how to raise their kids. We shouldn't be intruding into people's private lives.

Charles Dean: The debate over spanking and corporal punishment will continue, among parents and in the courts. In Dale Clover's case, he could get up to five years in prison if convicted of child abuse. I'm Charles Dean.

LISTEN FOR DETAILS
(Repeat Listen for Main Ideas)

MAKE INFERENCES

Excerpt One

Tyler Robinson: I want my children to learn right from wrong, but not out of fear. Spanking teaches children to be afraid of their parents, not respect them. I want my children to think of me as a friend, you know, someone they can talk with about problems.

Charles Dean: Robinson also thinks it teaches kids to use violence to solve problems.

Tyler Robinson: That's not a lesson I want to teach my children. I don't want my kids to hit anyone, so I don't hit them. . . .

Excerpt Two

Rhonda Moore: It's a parent's job to set clear limits, and spanking helps kids understand those limits. . . .

. . . Now, when I spank my kids, I always talk to them before and after, and explain why I'm spanking them. They understand that I'm doing this because I love them, not because I want to hurt them.

Excerpt Three

Beverly Lau: . . .The best way to teach them how to behave is to get them to say what they did wrong and to think of what they should've done instead. We call this active problem solving and we need to show our children how to do it. There still needs to be a consequence for the misbehavior. But it should be a consequence that makes sense. . . .

2B. LISTENING TWO: *Parents' Rights vs. Children's Rights*

Professor: OK. What I'd like to do today is look at the issue of spanking and corporal punishment as an issue of rights—the rights of parents versus the rights of children.

First, let's look at the rights of parents. Now, in most situations, parents have the right to raise their children the way they want. The law controls some things, like they may have to send their kids to school, but it doesn't usually control the details of family life, like how to discipline a child.

Now usually, under the law, it's illegal to hit someone else, right? OK. So if I hit a stranger walking down the street, that's illegal and I can be arrested. But many laws make an exception for parents disciplining their children—as long as the violence isn't extreme. Parents have the right to spank their children.

OK, let's look at the rights of the child now. Over the past hundred years, there has been more emphasis around the world on human rights. Human rights is the idea that all people—men and women, young and old—are equal and should be treated equally.

So, under this view, spanking violates the human rights of a child. The question is, why is it illegal to hit people in general, but OK to hit your own child?

Well, let's look at this: In response to this question, several countries around the world have made it illegal for parents to spank their children. The first country was Sweden, which passed a law in 1979 against the corporal punishment of children. And since then, a total of 18 countries have passed similar laws.

Now, in addition, the United Nations recommended that *all* countries pass laws to make corporal punishment of children illegal. As a matter of fact, in a recent report, the UN explains their position by saying: "Hitting people is wrong—and children are people too."

So you can see the two points of view on the issue of spanking: the rights of the parents to discipline their children the way they think is best, versus the human rights of children, the right to be free from violence. OK. Now let's look at the laws in different countries against corporal punishment . . . .

3C. SPEAKING

PRONUNCIATION: *Final s and z*

Exercise 3

abuse (verb)	rice
lose	plays
piece / peace	niece
ice	advise
fears	race

THE PHONETIC ALPHABET

Consonant Symbols

/b/	**b**e		/t/	**t**o
/d/	**d**o		/v/	**v**an
/f/	**f**ather		/w/	**w**ill
/g/	**g**et		/y/	**y**es
/h/	**h**e		/z/	**z**oo, bu**s**y
/k/	**k**eep, **c**an		/θ/	**th**anks
/l/	**l**et		/ð/	**th**en
/m/	**m**ay		/ʃ/	**sh**e
/n/	**n**o		/ʒ/	vi**s**ion, A**s**ia
/p/	**p**en		/tʃ/	**ch**ild
/r/	**r**ain		/dʒ/	**j**oin
/s/	**s**o, **c**ircle		/ŋ/	lo**ng**

Vowel Symbols

/ɑ/	f**a**r, h**o**t		/iy/	**we**, m**ea**n, f**ee**t
/ɛ/	m**e**t, s**ai**d		/ey/	d**ay**, l**a**te, r**ai**n
/ɔ/	t**a**ll, b**ou**ght		/ow/	**go**, l**ow**, c**oa**t
/ə/	s**o**n, **u**nder		/uw/	t**oo**, bl**ue**
/æ/	c**a**t		/ay/	t**i**me, b**uy**
/ɪ/	sh**i**p		/aw/	h**ou**se, n**ow**
/ʊ/	g**oo**d, c**ou**ld, p**u**t		/oy/	b**oy**, c**oi**n

CREDITS

Photo Credits: Page 1 Case study courtesy of GlaxoSmithKline Singapore and Ogilvy & Mather Singapore; **Page 9** ElectraGraphics, Inc.; **Page 10** (top) Courtesy of Saatchi & Saatchi Australia, (bottom left) Courtesy of Saatchi & Saatchi Australia, (bottom right) Courtesy of Conill New York; **Page 19** Pat Wellenbach/AP Images; **Page 20** Alberto Ruggieri/Illustration Works/Corbis; **Page 22** Brad Killer/iStockphoto.com; **Page 35** Pierre Verdy/Getty Images; **Page 36** (top left) Shutterstock, (top middle) Shutterstock, (top right) Shutterstock, (bottom) Pierre Verdy/Getty Images; **Page 37** Pierre Verdy/Getty Images; **Page 47** Lisette Le Bon/SuperStock; **Page 51** (top) Ronnie Kaufman/Corbis, (bottom left) Spencer Grant/Photo Researchers, Inc., (bottom middle) Tony Freeman/PhotoEdit, (bottom right) Getty Images; **Page 54** Aldo Murillo/iStockphoto.com; **Page 56** Stockbyte/Getty Images; **Page 73** Keren Su/Corbis; **Page 74** Anup Shah/naturepl.com; **Page 89** (top) Shutterstock, (bottom) David R. Frazier Photolibrary, Inc./Alamy; **Page 93** Spencer Grant / PhotoEdit; **Page 94** Photograph by Michael Pateman; **Page 111** (left) Emilio Ereza/SuperStock, (middle) Thinkstock/Jupiterimages, (right) Andersen Ross/Getty Images; **Page 115** Kamilla Mathisen/iStockphoto.com; **Page 118** Bettmann/Corbis; **Page 122** (left) Construction Photography/Corbis, (right) Randy Faris/Corbis; **Page 127** Shutterstock; **Page 131** Zigy Kaluzny-Charles Thatcher/Getty Images; **Page 135** IT Stock International/Jupiterimages; **Page 140** Shutterstock; **Page 157** Louie Balukoff/AP Images; **Page 174** Creatas/Jupiterimages; **Page 176** Brand X/SuperStock.

Listening Selections and Text Credits: Page 22 Music: Scheming Weasel (slower version), Kevin MacLeod (incompetech.com). Licensed under Creative Commons "Attribution 3.0" http://creativecommons.org/licenses/by/3.0/; **Page 38** "Ultrarunner Jay Batchen." Podcast presented by www.EndurancePlanet.com. Tim Borquin, host. June 10, 2005; **Page 96** Audio program that accompanies this text courtesy of Rounder Records, Corp., One Camp Street, Cambridge, Massachusetts 02140 U.S.A.; **Page 115** "Urban Homesteaders" produced and reported by Karen Brown, WFCR, Amherst, Massachusetts. © 2007 by Karen Brown. Used by permission; **Page 149** "What Makes a Marriage Work?" Copyright © 2007 Pew Research Center. All Rights reserved. http://pewresearch.org/pubs/526/marriage-parenthood; **Page 155** "Personal Carbon Footprint" Radio report produced and reported by Curt Nickisch; **Page 169** Figures 1 and 2: U.S. Carbon Dioxide Information Analysis Center; Figure 3: Adapted from Nationmaster http://www.nationmaster.com/graph/tra_mot_veh-transportation-motor-vehicles; **Page 171** Figure 5: "Trends in natural disasters." UNEP/GRID-Arendal Maps and Graphics Library. 2005. UNEP/GRID-Arendal. 28 Sep 2007. http://maps.grida.no/go/graphic/trends-in-natural-disasters. Emmanuelle Bournay, Cartographer. UNEP/GRID-Arendal. Used by permission; **Page 172** Figure 6: Jeremy L. Weiss and Jonathan Overpeck. Environmental Studies Laboratory, Department of Geosciences, University of Arizona

Illustration Credits: Aphik Diseño, **Pages 112, 151**; Paul Hampson, **Pages 11, 152, 166**; Mapping Specialists, Ltd., **Page 172**; Derek Mueller, **Pages 13, 95, 107**; Dusan Petricic, **Pages 28, 53, 98, 173**; Gary Torrisi, **Pages 68, 170**.

Notes

Notes